The City of London
A Financial and Commercial History

Robert Gibson-Jarvie

Published by
Woodhead-Faulkner
in association with
Commercial Union Assurance Company Limited

Published by Woodhead-Faulkner Ltd
8 Market Passage, Cambridge CB2 3PF
in association with Commercial Union Assurance Company Ltd

First published 1979

© Commercial Union Assurance Company Limited/
Robert Gibson-Jarvie 1979

ISBN 0 85941 090 0

Text layout by Book Production Consultants

Typeset in Monotype Garamond by Bedford Typesetters Ltd

Printed and bound in Great Britain by
William Clowes & Sons Ltd, Beccles and London

Foreword

London has many faces and each has been described countless times in books, essays, diaries and *belles lettres*. This publication attempts the difficult task of unravelling the financial and commercial mysteries of the City of London, that ancient and magical square mile, by describing how its various components have developed over the centuries.

As Robert Gibson-Jarvie points out, a key to understanding the City is to realise its prosaic, fundamental *raison d'être* – the movement of merchandise. For centuries conveying raw materials and finished products from source to consumer has required expert arrangement, financing and insurance. To achieve this continuously against target datelines and with due response to availability of goods and fluctuating prices it has been necessary to develop a whole range of specialised institutions centralised at a convenient power base that makes up the City today.

The world-wide nature of the City's business and its maritime associations have added romantic spice to the mixture. Here everyday deals involving millions of pounds and affecting the lives of people in remote countries are still sometimes completed perhaps with nothing more formal than a handshake, since personal reputations and trust in a man's word have traditionally been iron-clad securities. Not by chance did the Stock Exchange adopt the motto 'My word is my bond.'

Anyone who has worked or lived in the City will know that, whilst steeped in history, it is no fossil but an extremely lively and forward-looking animal. If anything, it perhaps tends to take its past for granted, being more concerned with the ever-changing present-day money market and its new challenges. Thus a book like this we feel will be of equal value and interest to people in the City as it undoubtedly will be to the three million visitors who each year come to Britain's capital.

Commercial Union takes particular pride in sponsoring this book. It is a natural follow-up to David Crawford's *The City of London: Its Architectural Heritage*, which was published by Woodhead-Faulkner in association with ourselves in 1976.

As an international insurance group our roots go back to 1696 when the Hand in Hand Fire and Life Insurance Society was born in Tom's Coffee House in St Martin's Lane. This, the oldest surviving insurance society in the world, is now part of a group whose parent company, Commercial Union Assurance, was founded in the City in 1861 by commercial interests following the Great Tooley Street Fire. Its headquarters remains in the City today.

Victor Head
Co-ordinator, Group Communications,
Commercial Union Assurance Company Ltd

Contents

Acknowledgements

The author wishes to acknowledge the generous and invaluable assistance of his many friends and counsellors in the City during the writing of this book, particularly that of Charles Clay, formerly Director General of the Accepting Houses Committee; Professor Hugh Cockerell, OBE, of the City University; Jeffrey Frost of the Committee on Invisible Exports; John Hunsworth, Director of Banking Information at the Committee of London Clearing Bankers; Anthony Southorn of the British Bankers Association; Colin Williams of the City Communications Centre; the British Insurance Association; the Chartered Insurance Institute; the Federation of Commodity Associations; Lloyd's of London; the Port of London Authority; and the Stock Exchange.

Grateful thanks for supplying the illustrations on the pages indicated are due to the following: the Bank of England, pages 41, 122; Trustees of the British Museum, pages 15, 22, 36, 44, 51, 60, 70; Coutts & Co., page 42; Fotomas Index, pages 81, 107, 113; Lloyd's of London, pages 89, 91, 94; the London Gold Market, page 55; the London Metal Exchange, page 66; the Moscow Narodny Bank Ltd, page 117; the Museum of London, pages 11, 18, 19, 26, 29, 31, 32, 38, 47, 63, 76, 78, 83, 85, 102, 110 and jacket; the National Portrait Gallery, page 59.

List of Illustrations

List of Illustrations

CHAPTER ONE

The City in Perspective

Unlike many other capitals, London, inside the compass of a single city, combines the seat of government with the country's banking and commercial headquarters and with a major centre of trade. It is one of the most complete capitals of the world.

Within this compass there exists side by side a whole range of individually identifiable segments, each devoted to one particular aspect of commerce and many still preserving their own corporate personality and traditions. Banking and other financial services, insurance, the Stock Exchange and the commodity markets all rub shoulders within the small area of the City proper – the Square Mile. Although modern handling methods and transport techniques are causing the Port and the markets in physical goods to be dispersed to neighbouring centres where access is easier, the management and direction of many of these trades, notably shipping and forwarding, remains within its own accepted and traditional part of the City.

Today this small area is bounded on the north by the street named London Wall and the brooding ramparts of the Barbican. On the east, fragments of the Roman wall (some revealed intriguingly as part of the interior walls of the basements of office buildings) can be seen, and then come the intricate worlds of Whitechapel and the markets beyond Houndsditch. To the west, the border lies at Temple Bar, though its fine gateway is now re-erected and in a somewhat sad state outside London; here the two worlds of the Law and the Press coincide in location and in their own ineffable atmosphere. Above all in importance, to the south the frontier is most dramatically drawn by the Thames itself: the prime and historic justification for the whole concentration. It is after all no more than a truism that all the world's great cities are built astride rivers.

Bearing in mind both the length of London's known history to date – well over a millennium – and the range of activities of a financial nature encompassed by the Square Mile, a single work doing full justice to each and every detail would be so massive as to daunt even the most intrepid reader. What, therefore, is to be left out? Very little, it is to be hoped; though unavoidably many of the finer points may only be sketched in.

With but a few exceptions, the majority of the individual specialisations that make up the whole intricate network of the financial and related activities carried on in the City are an open book only to those whose daily work takes them there. To the rest (including many who are themselves 'something in the City') they are almost as arcane as the magic of Merlin.

Ropemaker Street, Tenter Street, Tokenhouse Yard and French Ordinary Court are names redolent of antique commerce. Though they no longer literally define the businesses carried on there – indeed Tenter Street exists now only as a name on a plaque within the precincts of Britannic House – they serve as educational and rather charming examples of some of the separate domains within the whole: cordage, weaving, the Exchequer and the import of wine. Today the various trades tend to be concentrated in their own areas, some of whose names still give an indication of the business done there.

The key to a proper appreciation of the way the City of London works is the principle that all these cities within the City aim in their various ways at the same goal – the movement of merchandise. Raw materials become finished goods and progress from producer to processor to consumer. This movement has to be executed, financed, insured and made as continuous as possible both as to the availability of the goods, and as to their price, on the due date. This, then, was the prime motive of all the countless highly specialised houses which made up the City of yesterday. It remains so for the fewer, larger and more integrated, yet no less expert, institutions operating there today.

How was it that this highly centralised organism came into being in the first place, and how has it developed over the years? To seek answers to these questions is both interesting, to those with a penchant for history, and important if we are to glean a proper understanding of what the City is all about, what the future may hold in store for it, and what example it has to offer.

> '*Before the Roman came to Rye, or out to Severn strode,*
> *The rolling English drunkard made the rolling English road.*'

With his inimitable feeling for the spirit of the thing, G. K. Chesterton, that most English of poets, caught the essential force behind what might otherwise appear an almost totally haphazard progress. Probably less directed by ale than by the need to find a route from one point to another, which could be traversed by herd or flock over awkward terrain, the trading routes of England meandered in what today would seem an almost perverse manner. Until the Romans came there was no civil engineering and the country was crossed and divided by watercourses and swamps which had to be bypassed or forded.

When the Romans arrived they found a large, swampy and generally difficult area around the Thames roughly between a high point at the ford and stepping stones at Staines (Stennes), and the lowest crossing by the legendary bridge (or ford) near the present Westminster Bridge. Further downstream the Thames debouched into a very wide and complicated tidal estuary. This provided the makings of an important maritime gateway from London to the European mainland.

So the roads in the east of the country led to, and in due course over, the great eastward-flowing river and in so doing provided the nexus of both

Roman London, about AD 120: reconstruction drawing by Alan Sorrell

internal and outward, seagoing, trade routes on an amazingly comprehensive scale.

The Romans paid two visits to Britain, of which the first under Julius Caesar in the year 55 BC was in the nature of a reconnaissance in force. The second invasion, in the year AD 43, marked the commencement of something really significant in economic and social terms, as well as being a settlement in the true sense of the word. What in fact happened was that this outstandingly capable and efficient city state of Rome, developed in the Mediterranean tradition of such states, had reached a point in its own economic development when even a group of less than hospitable islands in the north was seen to be an ingredient in the unavoidable process of expansion. Colonisation, as distinct from simple raiding and plundering, was the aim, and it was achieved with very great thoroughness.

In order to gain such an end, the Romans had first to establish communications on a scale rather more businesslike than that provided by the existing rambling lanes and ridgeways. Their aim was to settle and exploit the hinterland and, before doing so, to deal with whatever organised opposition they might find lying in wait for them.

Topography was to dictate the first step towards solving their problems. The marshes upon which the legions found themselves led them westwards upstream along the south bank of the Thames, while the nearest and most immediately important of the opposing tribes was to be found in the southern half of the East Anglian bulge, in and around Colchester. These people, called by the Romans the Catuvellauni, reputedly crossed the river fairly regularly by a bridge in the course of their own commerce with the Continent. Where this bridge (or it may have been a traversable ford) was located we have little evidence. However, a quantity of weapons and various accoutrements have been recovered over the years and these demonstrate fairly convincingly that the river was crossed at more than one place within the limits of the present-day London – both by the natives of those parts and by the Romans.

With London as their military headquarters, the Romans advanced outwards, creating totally new 'surveyor's roads' which ran direct from point to point without regard to following a favourable contour. As each of these routes was lengthened, pushing further into the hinterland, settlements and military camps sprang up along the way, in many cases forming the nucleus of more permanent townships. But the centre of this network remained at London, which became a trading and military capital commanding an advanced system of communications over dry land into a hitherto little penetrated hinterland. On its eastern flank this capital possessed a major maritime outlet to Europe and the world.

Further emphasis, if such were needed, of the growing significance of London to the native British came with the bloody and almost successful revolt of the Iceni under their queen, Boadicea. At a time when the bulk of the Roman army of occupation was absent to the west, Boadicea led her forces in a cataclysmic descent upon a largely undefended city. The story goes that the Iceni, streaming down the road and the adjacent valleys of the Rodings from Colchester and the surrounding area, attacked and razed London with ferocity. The significance of the attack is that the city had become the symbol of centralisation and as such an emotive, as well as a military target in the eyes of Boadicea, who saw herself and her people reduced to a satellite role.

Following this uprising, which was taken so seriously in Rome that the then governor of Britain was recalled, a major programme of fortification was undertaken. The wall around London and the barracks at its north-western corner are still easily traced for much of their length – especially after bombing in the Second World War revealed large sections which had previously been obscured by, and largely built into, later work. The barracks itself covered the area which lies to the south of the Barbican development, and its *via principalis* lay along what is now Wood Street.

The Roman occupation of England (and their incursion into the lowlands of Scotland) was an exercise in colonisation and political stabilisation. As such it had a profound effect on such matters as the administration of justice and the beginnings of the establishment of a more organised and cohesive society. Coin came into common use as the means of exchange, and as a yardstick for putting a value on goods; the coins themselves having an intrinsic value in terms of their weight and metal content. The concept of paper money backed by reserves was not a part of their system, so that it was by way of improved communications and the greater stability afforded by being a colony of a great power that the Roman influence on the development of London as a centre was most noticeable.

The relationship between colonisers and colonised became in time a reasonably harmonious one, although the legions were never completely without military preoccupations along the northern and western boundaries. In many instances ties were made at family level by marriage and by the adoption of native children into Roman households.

If the picture in Britain was becoming a more tranquil one, this was far from the case in Rome itself. Internecine strife at home led to indecisiveness and corruption. This either spread directly outwards to the colonial pos-sessions or else so undermined the authority (and reduced the resources) of local administrators as to make the position of many of them no longer tenable. So it was with Britain. The outcome was that not only the legions, but also a considerable body of able and honest civilian administrators were either withdrawn, or rendered powerless to continue in government over their allotted territories.

The process of consolidation had not gone far enough for it to have any real permanence. Once more the old tribal and local loyalties asserted themselves as the Roman influence dwindled and their methods (and even their buildings and installations) fell into disuse. The Roman legal system has never been adopted in England, though Scots law has much that is derived from Roman law. As to matters financial, it is an interesting side-light on the Romans that they never evolved any system of numerals, making use of a complicated adaptation of their alphabet instead. The main legacy of their occupation which endured for some four centuries was a magnificent web of internal and external communications with London at its centre – a fortified town of great strategic importance.

Not a great deal is known about London after the departure of the Romans. Its location and the high degree of its development as a centre must have contributed to its continuance as an entity in its own right, but it does seem that for a time at least the city suffered a sharp decline in importance. The country found itself divided between warring factions and, in the eastern regions at any rate, the subject of invasions from across the sea.

It was during this strife-torn and little-documented period that the Saxon settlements were established. It would appear that they, too, came first as raiders, but were encouraged in time to cooperate with local chieftains as well disciplined and able soldiers and workers. (In Germany it is still said of an energetic and efficient man that he 'works like a Saxon'.) Gradually the Saxons became the rulers of the country, which was divided into separate kingdoms.

By the seventh century London had become the chief town of the East Saxons, but was detached along with Middlesex in the eighth century to become a part of the central kingdom of Mercia. Ethelbert of Kent founded the first Saxon cathedral, St Paul's, in what was part of the progressive acceptance of Christianity by the hitherto pagan Saxons. One reads how Bishop Helmstan of Winchester was consecrated 'in the illustrious place, built by the skill of the ancient Romans, called throughout the world the great city of London'.

There followed a turbulent time with London the not always unwilling object of a series of invasions and counter-invasions – twice by the Danes,

The Lord Mayor's Court Office in the nineteenth century: engraving by
T. Hosmer Shepherd

once (a counter-invasion, this) by the West Saxons under Alfred, and finally
the occupation by the Normans under William after his defeat of the
defending forces in the Battle of Hastings in 1066.

During the years preceding the Norman Conquest, London became
firmly established as the trading and political centre of the country, and this
progress is worth following. The court and seat of government remained
outside the City, which stoutly proclaimed its individuality and indeed is
today governed with a degree of autonomy which is on occasion the object
of envy.

During the years of strife which followed the departure of the Romans,
London retained its cohesion as a township (to put it at its lowest degree),
and the people of London developed their own methods of self-government.
A distinct, and in a sense patrician, class of thegns established itself, wielding
considerable authority over the citizenry in general and over the administration of justice in particular. The folkmoot met regularly three times each
year on the high ground to the north-east of St Paul's, and every citizen

was duty-bound to be in attendance. For dealing with civil causes, as distinct from matters of public law and order, the hustings assembled frequently and regularly. (It is a curious instance of the changing significance of words, that we now think of the hustings in terms of the general frenzy of mobile loudspeakers and the posturing of rival candidates in a political election.)

The ealdormen, or elders, in turn sat separately in their own private courts of justice: one for each of the wards into which the City was divided for administrative purposes. Today, the Aldermen are still elected by the voters of their respective wards, to form the senior cadre of the City's government in the Court of Common Council. The open wardmoot exists even now as a forum to be convened for public discussion and debate.

The establishment of London as the political capital of the country was a gradual affair. In Saxon and early medieval times the court followed the king as he moved about his domain. The concept of a fixed and permanent capital was then quite alien to the countries of western Europe. However, a measure of the importance attaching to London as the political centre of the country in later Saxon times was the right claimed by its people to elect the king. This right was exercised on more than one occasion, when either the deceased king had no heir or a choice between rival heirs apparent was necessary. When succession was undoubted and acceptable, or when the new king proclaimed himself from a position of military superiority, things were a little different.

Indeed, the strategic and political importance which London had drawn to itself could, and on occasion did, work to the disadvantage of its citizens. After Cnut the Dane had established himself firmly as King of England, he felt sufficiently secure to effect a reduction in his armed forces and he paid off his invasion fleet in the year 1017. For this, the unfortunate Londoners were compelled to subscribe no less than £10,500. After the death of Cnut and then, in 1042, of Harthacnut (his only legitimate son), it was once more the people of London who were responsible for filling the vacant throne. By popular acclaim Edward, son of Ethelred II, was elected king and so the older dynasty found itself restored with the end of the male Danish line. In passing, a curiously human touch is added to this sequence of events, since it is recorded that Harthacnut – still only in his twenties – collapsed and died 'as he stood at his drink' at the wedding feast of a companion.

Though king, Edward probably wielded less influence over affairs than did Harold, son of Earl Godwine of Wessex. Godwine was ambitious and extremely powerful – to the extent that in 1051 he was forced into exile by Edward, who regarded him as a source of danger. In the next year, however, we see Godwine leading an expeditionary force up the Thames and actually being permitted by the Londoners to pass through the arches of London Bridge, where he routed the king's fleet and compelled Edward to treat with him. This brought Godwine and his son Harold back into prominence. In consequence when Edward died in January 1066, and was buried in his own recently consecrated Westminster Abbey, Harold was chosen king and straightaway crowned in that same Abbey. His was to be but a short reign, as he was killed in the Battle of Hastings later that year when William of Normandy landed in England.

William marched with all despatch to London, for such was its established importance that he considered it essential to occupy and control it. He was met by resistance at first, but was able (not without some savagery inflicted on the less fortunate citizens living on the south bank of the river) to exact a more or less complete submission. The lasting monument to this cataclysmic event is the massive and beautiful White Tower built by William as the first edifice in the Tower of London.

But it was not all a matter of oppression. William signed a charter – which still survives in the Guildhall – in which amongst other concessions to the City he pledged himself to retain 'its laws and customs as they were in Edward's time'.

In the twelfth century we hear for the first time of the Mayor of London, who appears to have been the City's spokesman in matters where the Crown and City were in discussion, if not actually in dispute. The first Mayor was Henry Fitz Aylwin, a merchant. One of his tasks was to persuade Londoners to contribute towards raising the ransom money to secure the release of King Richard I, the 'Lionheart', from captivity in Germany, where he had been seized on his return from a crusade to the Holy Land.

The annually elected office of Mayor dates from a charter of the disastrous King John in 1215 when he sought, rather desperately and not very successfully, to win the citizens of London to his side before being compelled to subscribe to Magna Carta that same year.

The raising of money from the City by the Crown, whether by voluntary subscription or as the result of some form of near-blackmail became from this period a firm tradition. Today, as we shall see in a little more detail later, that tradition is still followed in the sale and purchase of gilt-edged securities – units of government debt.

Meanwhile, the constitution of the ruling class within the City was radically altering. Those taking part in the various commercial activities began to create for themselves formal associations for their mutual protection and benefit. Most of these activities were concerned with the distribution

Fifteenth century silver seal and impression of the Brewers' Company, showing the Assumption of Our Lady

and marketing within Britain of merchandise, which was largely imported from overseas. The associations coalesced into very close-knit units, the 'Misteries', and were the prototypes of the livery companies as we know them today.

Once established, the livery companies assumed an important role in the government of the City, backed as they were by accumulations of wealth derived from expanding trade. Some of these companies held key positions in the distribution of staple items and in the allocation of the officials responsible for their supervision. Today most, if not all, of these functions are superseded, or in other hands, but the companies continue to put their wealth to good use in such charitable and educational areas as the endowment of schools and hospitals and in the sponsoring of apprenticeships. Their influence over the City's affairs has become more indirect, though it is still far from insignificant.

In many cases there is still a traceable link with modern businesses and trades – for example the Coachmakers have an affinity with the motor industry and the Fanmakers with plastics – and, aside from any personal membership of the liveries of those active in the industry, the companies' periodic foregatherings provide opportunities for meetings on common ground. In this context, the dinners with their ritual are a long way from being merely the rather splendid anachronisms which some make them out to be.

As medieval turbulence and the recurring strife between an autocratic City and an equally autocratic king gradually gave place to a less fraught relationship, the government and the way of living of the City continued its own independent way. The Guildhall, built between 1411 and 1440 by the square still called Aldermanbury, remains the seat of the City's own governing body. The building received fire damage during the Second World War but has been lovingly restored, whilst of two recent annexes, one may be described as carefully traditional, and the other, the more recent, is a bold essay in reconciling renaissance with contemporary architectural styles. Curiously enough, the Mansion House, which is the Lord Mayor's official residence, was not built until the eighteenth century.

The City possesses its own police force with headquarters in a rather odd looking building in Wood Street, which in a sense goes full circle to the time when the Roman disciplinary force was quartered there. Of the departments of the City Police, the Company Fraud Squad merits mention

The Guildhall in the eighteenth century

separately as what is arguably the most expert and sophisticated force of its kind, and which on more than one occasion has lent aid to other investigatory organisations in other places and on matters other than purely financial malpractice.

So the position of the City as a financial and trade centre became firmly established, and also its curious position as a semi-autonomous body alongside, yet in many ways separate from, the seat of national government in Westminster. Wars and religious persecutions, along with the natural and timeless urge to seek fresh fields and pastures new, were still to play a major part in the progress of financial London. Invasions – albeit of a more pacific nature than heretofore – were still to be a feature of that progress, as the City became more cosmopolitan. New citizens brought with them new skills, finding London an agreeable as well as a practical centre for their operations. Not for nothing were Lombard Street and Old Jewry so named and names such as Wolff, Schweder, Rothschild and Czarnikow (to cite but a few) have become familiar in their specialised fields. These new incursions are best described and fitted into the perspective of the whole in the chapters to follow, when we consider in depth the various interdependent institutions and skills which together constitute the City as we know it, and to whose origin and subsequent development each new influx has made its own special contribution.

CHAPTER TWO

The Port of London

Such is the parochial nature of much of the City's activities, with all but self-contained communities jostling with their neighbours while remaining intent on their own affairs, that it is not always obvious, even to those who work there, that London is a busy port. And without doubt it was its existence as a port from very early days which went furthest to establish the City as a trading, and later as a banking and financial, centre. To produce anything as concentrated and yet as diversified as the City of London some sort of common stimulus had to be provided, and this stimulus came with the development of the river and its shores into what was to become Britain's most important and busiest port.

In this sense London was trebly fortunate. First, the Thames flowed out to the sea at precisely the point best suited for access to and from the northern and western European mainland with its own great arteries of the Gironde, Rhine and Elbe and further north the Baltic Sea itself. In the second place London was situated at the lowest point at which the river could conveniently be crossed by bridge or ford; although the northern bank consisted of relatively solid ground, the southern side consisted until quite recent times of marshes not easily traversable. Finally, this very fact meant that the lower reaches of the estuary were sufficiently awkward to navigate as to deter the less adept invader without unduly hazarding the vessels of seamen who were familiar with its tides and moods.

Now, if the Upper Pool and the warehouses fronting it have lost their original status (yet found a new purpose as amenities rather than as centres of commerce), the ancillary businesses that sprang up in close proximity remain concentrated in this small area.

Exports from London to the Continent are known to have been considerable even before the Roman occupation. The Catuvellauni, for example, were exporters of hunting dogs amongst other less glamorous items.

The Custom House and the Port of London: aquatint by Pugin and Rowlandson

Minerals, too, were shipped out in exchange for the produce of areas as far distant as the southern shores of the Mediterranean; and the Romans called England the 'Granary of the North', in respect for her considerable exports of cereals.

With their gift for organisation, the Romans did much, not only to regulate the trade flowing in and out of London, but also to improve and extend the port's facilities to link up with the network of roads which they constructed. At this time, too, we hear of the levying of customs duties on some items of produce. Recent archaeological digs have uncovered much Roman work along what were the banks of the river, though these are now well inland of the present embankments. Examples of this narrowing of the river may readily be seen in the watergate of the Earl of Buckingham's house standing at the landward extremity of the gardens by Embankment underground station, and in the steps and fragment of landing stage in the gardens adjacent to the Air Ministry building.

The earliest quays and jetties were concentrated in the area close to where the rivers Fleet and Walbrook joined the Thames, and the remains of a Saxon ship have recently been uncovered there. However, the majority of the larger vessels entering the Thames anchored in mid-stream and discharged their cargo via lighters which brought it ashore. The Thames lighterman has for long been an important figure on the river.

During the turbulent Saxon period and that of the repeated Danish invasions, London contrived to remain active as a port and as a safe storage place for produce. This was probably as much due to its fortunate location at the head of a difficult and complicated estuary as to its defences against an attack from landward. One of the earliest of the stone quays to be constructed was that which now forms Queenhithe close to Southwark Bridge. This originated with the gift of the land to Bishop Ethelred by King Alfred. First styled 'Ethelredshithe', the quay was renamed when it became the property of Matilda, wife of Henry I. Another very early quay or 'hithe' was that at Billingsgate, where the northern end of a cross-river ferry was situated.

England was a very considerable exporter of wool as well as grain. A proportion of the wool trade was carried on from London with the clip from the Thames valley and at least part of that from the north Oxfordshire plain, although ports in East Anglia, notably Boston, probably handled more tonnage collectively. However, by far the greater part of the shipping in and out of London was foreign. In 1275 Edward I introduced a tax on the export of wool, and in order to make its collection easier he decreed that wool from England might be landed only at specified places, commencing with Brabant in the Low Countries. This brought more of the trade to London as the most conveniently situated port of egress, and the Brabant 'staple' was greeted with glee by those London merchants who were approved as merchants of the staple. However, there were other complications – wars had to be financed, for example – which meant that the tax was increased at the royal whim and eventually a new staple was more or less forced upon the impecunious Edward III with Calais as the mainland port of entry; the trade was confined to the Merchants of the Staple, putting them in a comfortable monopoly position.

One consequence of the export tax was – perhaps not very surprisingly since the evidence is that it was a severe impost – that the wool trade itself declined. (An interesting aside here is that the poet Geoffrey Chaucer was at the time a customs officer in London and one of his responsibilities must have been the gathering of the wool tax.) It was soon found more profitable to weave the wool into cloth, and then to export the woven material. This was cheaper for Continental customers than locally woven cloth made from wool imported from England, to the price of which the English export tax had been added. Thus originated Britain's cloth trade and thus was created yet another spur to mercantile activity in the Port of London.

Here we may make mention of one of those 'peaceful invasions' the occurrence or aftermath of which has left its imprint on the financial and commercial pattern. In 1404 a group of English merchants formed to exploit the trade potential of northern Europe, whence came not only grain and furs but other essentials such as timber, hemp, tallow and materials for shipbuilding. Known as the Baltic Adventurers, they were granted a monopoly of the trade with this area. Unfortunately for them they were unable to compete with the already established and highly sophisticated Hanseatic League of north German merchants, who operated from both Baltic and North Sea ports. The life-span of the Baltic Adventurers was a short one, and by the third quarter of the fifteenth century the Hanseatic League was once more in sole command of the northern European trade.

For some centuries the Hansards or 'Easterlings', as they were known, had a base in London and established themselves in their Staelhof (Staple-house), which became anglicised as the Stillyard or Steelyard. This was a store of considerable dimensions built by the river's edge where Cannon Street station now stands. The Easterlings – from whose name 'sterling' is said to have derived – and the Lombard financiers from Italy, of whom we shall read more in a later chapter, were amongst the first of the several generations of *emigrés* from the European mainland to settle in the City and bring their special skills with them.

Resentment grew at the rather exclusive nature of the Easterlings' way of going about things, for they lived within the Stillyard and closed its gates on the rest of the City. Their monopoly ended effectively in the mid sixteenth century and later Queen Elizabeth I ordained that the Stillyard be closed down and that the Easterlings themselves quit the country. The ending of the Hansard monopoly gave the impetus for the expansion of the English Merchant Venturers' activities, and encouraged the formation of the Eastland Company which took over from the banished Hansards.

Of the chartered companies which did so much to increase the overseas trade in and out of London, mention must be made of the first to be recorded – the Muscovy Company. This was set up following a voyage to the White Sea by Willoughby and Chancellor in 1553. Willoughby was lost, but his companion landed at Archangel and was granted an interview in Moscow by no less a figure than the Tsar Ivan the Terrible, who on this occasion belied his soubriquet and handed to the Englishman a letter to his king, Edward VI (who actually died just after Chancellor set sail). The company was granted its charter by Mary Tudor in 1555 with the rather splendid superscription of 'The Mysterie and Companie of the Merchant Adventurers for the Discoverie of Regions, Dominions, Islands and Places unknown'.

The Muscovy Company's monopoly, however, was not to be a long one, and in fact competition in the Baltic area from the newly formed Eastland Company as well as from independent venturers was not slow in coming. This was due in part at least to the revocation by the recently enthroned Queen Elizabeth of the law compelling all English merchants to ship goods in English bottoms, or in the case of imports to Britain in vessels belonging to the exporting country. Now the shipping business and all that led from it could again be truly international.

Perhaps the most renowned of the chartered companies was the East India Company – 'John Company'. This company was founded in 1600 to open up the trade route to the Indian subcontinent and the spice islands of the East Indies. The first charter was in fact signed by Queen Elizabeth on 31 December 1599 – the last day of the sixteenth century. The immediate cause of the company's formation was actually another phase in the continuing, unremitting trade war; this time with the Dutch who had succeeded the Hansards as England's leading rivals. The Dutch were at the time already active traders with the East Indies and therefore major importers into Europe of spices. There is a not very respectful saying that 'the fault with the Dutch is giving too little and asking too much'.

Be that as it may, in 1599 the price of imported pepper in London was increased from three to eight shillings per pound. This was too much for the London merchants to tolerate without some form of retaliation. A meeting was held with the Lord Mayor in the chair and as a result the East India Company was brought into being with its royal charter.

The first convoy of Indiamen sailed in 1600, under James Lancaster. They were away for two years and returned with a cargo of spices, predominantly pepper. (In the days before refrigeration, or even the ice-house, spices and pepper were of importance as aids to preserving foods as well as being used for flavouring, possibly to disguise any unpleasant taste should the preservation process have been inadequate.)

The company went from strength to strength until it occupied a unique and quasi-governmental position in India itself. Its history was not without vicissitudes, though. Towards the end of the eighteenth century we read of its financial problems, accompanied by unsympathetic comment by merchants, by now resentful of this sprawling monopoly over such a large and extremely lucrative area. But the company's charter was again renewed and its monopoly was sustained until 1830. Very shortly after this the

company ceased trading, on the grounds that without the protection from competition which it had previously enjoyed, it could no longer operate at a profit. Though the passing of the company may have appeared an example of going not with a bang but a whimper, we should remember the enormous influence and achievement of 'John Company' over his two centuries of existence.

The confused and warlike epoch spanning the interval between the Norman and Elizabethan periods was in many ways a beneficial one as far as the City and the Port were concerned. In those days merchantmen tended to double up as men-of-war as occasion demanded and it was therefore a matter of some importance for the monarch to have a reasonably large and up-to-date merchant fleet available should need arise.

On a number of occasions the City Fathers were able to gain further privileges – more often than not these were lucrative – in return for pledges of support for the Crown. Before the days of overall taxation the king needed the support of the richest community in the land. In this fashion a series of charters was drawn up, each one conceding a part of what had been the absolute prerogative of the Crown over the river. As examples, the right to pack and weigh cargoes, to inspect them if liable to customs duty, to gauge wine and to garble (clean and sort) spices all added to the City's prestige and to its corporate income. The guilds or livery companies all came to specialise in one or several of these activities; though how they were parcelled out seems a little illogical. We find, for example, that the Salters were concerned chiefly with the stocking of textiles, whilst the Grocers (not surprisingly) and the Chandlers (surprisingly) took most of the responsibility for the distribution of salt.

The earlier quays being in some cases above the first stone-built London Bridge, it was necessary to unload bulk cargo and transport it to the quays themselves in lighters which were capable of passing through the bridge's many narrow arches. Peter of Colechurch, who built this bridge, was buried beneath the chapel on the bridge. It is a commentary on the durability of the work of his masons that their bridge stood until 1830, and even then the work of its demolition took nearly two years! Work on the construction of the first stone bridge began in 1176 and it was completed, with nineteen arches, in 1209, having been financed by the wool tax. London Bridge has always held a special position in the eyes of the City and even today the Bridge Fund is one of the Corporation's several special funds: from this is still drawn any money necessary for the bridge's repair or maintenance.

A stone corbel from old London Bridge

London Bridge costs the ratepayer nothing, for which he has to thank his forebears who bequeathed a part of their wealth 'to God and the Bridge'.

And so the Thames maintained its position as London's widest street. 'A man would say that seeth the shipping there that it is, as it were, a very wood of trees disbranched to make glades and let in light . . .'

Indeed, in the Elizabethan period London was firmly established as the major English port for exports as well as for the discharge of cargoes from overseas. One half of the total customs revenue was contributed by shipping in and out of London. One of the consequences of this was that Her Majesty Elizabeth I, being displeased with the amount of revenue being collected, in 1559 appointed a Commission, whose function was to organise a system of 'legal quays' at which all imported goods were to be discharged during the hours of daylight. In the event, twenty wharves were designated legal quays – all situated between the Tower and London Bridge with less than 1,500 feet of berthing area between them. The congestion became considerable, and the owners of the quays were placed in a singularly fortunate position, only partly diminished by the approval of adjacent overflow or 'sufferance' wharves with limited customs privileges.

Inequitable as this undoubtedly was, the arrangement was nevertheless indirectly responsible for various benefits arising. Thomas Gresham, for example, found himself in a position financially to sponsor the building of the Royal Exchange (of which the first stone was laid in 1567) as the forerunner, did he but know it, of today's commodity markets. This new-found wealth shared amongst a few also gave rise to a whole range of little industries which were engaged in the making of the accessories to gracious living and which – at least until the Second World War – occupied their traditional places in the City.

Foreign wars inevitably influenced trade and often succeeded in promoting it to and from the Port. One such instance was the war between the Netherlands and Spain and, in particular, the sacking of Antwerp by the Duke of Parma's army in 1576. This destroyed the mercantile supremacy of that city and placed London directly in line to inherit it. From this time onwards London began to take an increasing share in the practice of entrepôt or third-country trading as distinct from direct import and export to and from our own shores.

Meanwhile, looking westwards, the first British settlement in America was founded in 1606 when three ships – all under 100 tons, be it noted – sailed from Blackwall under the command of Captain John Smith to set up the colony of Virginia. Later that century the formation of the Hudson's Bay Company was an event of equal if not greater significance. In June

1668 the *Nonsuch* and *Eaglet* sailed from Gravesend for Hudson's Bay in Canada. The *Nonsuch* survived the voyage and returned in the following year with a cargo of furs and skins from the Canadian hinterland. A company was promptly set up and received its charter at the hands of Charles II on 2 May 1670 with the King's cousin Prince Rupert as its first Governor. This was to prove a success story in every sense, and it is interesting to note that the Hudson's Bay Company, which is still active, holds its regular fur auctions in Beaver House, near Mansion House station, to this day.

With the setting-up of the legal quays, the larger ocean-going ships were forced, as we have already noted, to anchor in the stream further down-river. The East Indiamen at this time made use, as lighters for the transfer of their cargoes, of the first covered barges in use in the Port. The East India Company then had a wet dock built at Blackwall for the repair and refit of their ships whilst in London and this was actually the first non-tidal dock in the Thames, being fitted with gates to retain the water

A view of London Bridge in 1616, from an engraving by John Visscher

once a ship had been warped in. It was later incorporated into the new East India Dock itself.

After the Great Fire of 1666 had wreaked havoc among the still largely wooden quays and warehouses with their often inflammable contents, a special levy was placed on all coal discharging in the Port as a means of going some way towards covering the cost of the massive rebuilding programme. (Coal at the time was already a widely-used fuel and even then there were bitter complaints at the smoke and dirt which its use in open hearths engendered.)

Work on what are now the Surrey Docks on the south bank was put in hand after the grant of the Royal Assent in 1696, the Crown still holding the rights over all development on the riverside. This was a large undertaking, covering as it did some ten acres, and was first named the Howland Great Wet Dock, after the family from whose land it was excavated. It marked the beginning of a long era in which the traffic of the Port was expanded and more and more dock complexes within its precincts were constructed. The volume of trade in the Thames increased markedly during the eighteenth century as Britain's merchantmen ranged wider in their search for trade, notably to the West Indies. The Port's business continued to grow until by 1792 it was handling over £12 million of exports and nearly £15 million of imports, some 65 per cent of the total for the country as a whole.

The increasing trade brought its own problems, and congestion in the river (especially in and around the area of the Pool) became intolerable. Delays were taking place owing to goods having to remain on board lighters which were rarely adequately protected either against the weather or against the depredations of organised gangs of thieves. Indeed, one might almost say that a whole sub-commerce had arisen in the traffic – frequently with the active connivance of port and customs officers – in goods that were 'imported' by being lifted at night from the holds of the lighters or from open and inadequately guarded quaysides. The activities and composition of these gangs are probably more a part of a social than a financial history, but we might in passing pause and consider some of their names: the River Pirates, the Scuffle-Hunters, the Mudlarks and the Plunderers, not to mention the Light and the Heavy Horsemen!

The owners of the quays were naturally not too displeased at the ever-increasing amount of business coming their way and were in consequence unenthusiastic over any prospect of more quay space becoming available lest their jam become spread too thin. However, since by the end of the eighteenth century there was a real risk of business diverting from London

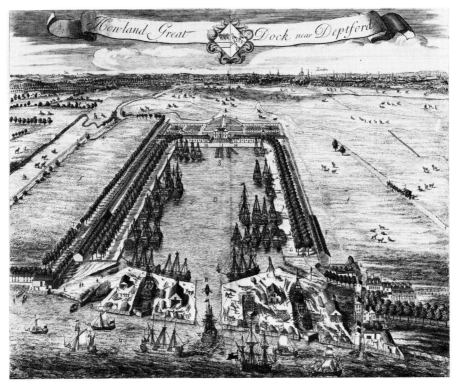

Howland Great Wet Dock, from an engraving by Thomas Badeslade about 1720

on account of its overcrowded state, a Parliamentary Committee was set up to look into the matter in 1796. As a result of its deliberations an Act was passed in 1799 authorising the construction of further docks in the curiously named Isle of Dogs. Not an island in the true sense, this is the area enclosed by the great sweep of the Thames comprising Limehouse Reach, Greenwich Reach and Blackwall Reach. The Royal Naval College and Hospital at Greenwich on the south bank (built on the site of Greenwich Palace, where Queen Elizabeth I was born) face Millwall at the 'island's' southern extremity. These new docks were to be used for the burgeoning West Indies trade, and were the nucleus of the West India and Millwall Docks complex.

The 1799 Act provided that all goods inwards from the West Indies and outwards towards them be handled in the new docks and – this is significant – that lightermen entering the docks for this purpose might do so without payment of dues. This 'Free Water Clause' in the Act was retained in all later legislation concerning dockland developments. The

A view of the proposed St Katharine's Dock, lithographed by T. M. Baynes about 1825

docks themselves are noteworthy in that within their precincts were constructed multi-storey covered warehouses whose integrity was maintained by armed security guards.

From then until the end of the nineteenth century further construction took place, following the example set by the West India Docks of having enclosed basins for ships to lie alongside combined with adequate warehousing close at hand. Of these, perhaps the most noteworthy today are the St Katharine's Dock and warehouse group below Tower Bridge, originally constructed for the wine trade in 1828. Now, the whole site is being developed into a pleasing sailing and yachting leisure centre.

The Port of London Authority itself, which now has sole responsibility for the river upwards to Teddington Lock (reputedly 'Tide End Town') at the end of the tidal river, was brought into being by an Act of Parliament of 1908.

Though it is not directly germane to a financial history, it would not be proper to conclude this brief survey of the Port without considering the shipbuilding activity there. As early as the time of Henry VIII there were royal dockyards at Deptford and Woolwich, of which the former became the chief shipbuilding and chandlery in the country for furnishing ships of the Royal Navy, a service which claims its origin in the fleet founded by King Alfred. The Deptford yard closed in 1869 after launching HMS *Druid*, its last ship. At Blackwall the East India Company built a number of its own ships, and several of the clippers for the China tea and the Australian wool trades were also constructed there. *Cutty Sark*, the last surviving clipper and a Clyde-built ship, is now maintained in dry dock at Greenwich; her name literally translated means, surprisingly enough, 'Short Shirt'.

The almost continually increasing activity and the diversity of the business carried on in the Port of London have over the centuries made a direct and important contribution to the growth of all the other services which stem from the business of a port. Without this central nucleus it is highly doubtful whether the commodity markets or the banking, financial and insurance network gathered in the City would ever have flourished to the same degree. And if it is with a measure of real regret that we watch the inevitable transfer of deep-water shipping and cargo handling elsewhere (much of it to the huge complex downstream at Tilbury) we may thank the river for providing the stimulus for all these other developments.

CHAPTER THREE

Banks and Banking in England

With the movement and exchange of goods must come the efficient transfer of money. Today, banking is so much a part of our everyday lives that it requires a stretch of the imagination to visualise a world where such an essential service was not immediately available to all who needed it. Yet the granting of credit and the transfer of wealth by documentary means took a great many years to develop to anything approaching present standards.

Of all the means towards achieving such an end, the bill of exchange ranks historically as the oldest; its existence can be traced back through many hundreds of years to the mercantile city states bordering the Mediterranean, and to older Middle Eastern civilisations before them.

It is known that the Romans used a form of bill of exchange, and it may be surmised that its use was not confined to the capital itself. However, if the Romans in Britain did make use of the bill, we find no record of the system surviving their departure. In Saxon and medieval times we know that coinage was in use, and there is ample evidence of a system of the minting of coins by licensed moneyers, whose monograms appear on the coins themselves. However, banking in the sense of the transfer of wealth, the granting of credit or the provision of a safe hoarding place for savings was not a feature of pre-Norman Britain.

Probably the first professional financiers in anything like significant numbers were the Jews, who came to England in the wake of William the Conqueror. They established themselves as a community in London, mainly in the area round Cheapside to which the street name of Old Jewry bears witness.

The Jews became prosperous though never secure. They had no recognised legal status; indeed they were effectively banned from activity in any sort of trade or manufacturing business, although they could and did own property. This restriction on the activities of the Jews resulted in their turning to the lending of money at a rate of interest as their chief source of income. In this they were remarkably successful, to the extent that by being in a position to offer finance to the king they were able to give themselves a measure of protection from the various sanctions imposed on them by a largely hostile native population.

Unfortunately the rapaciousness of certain monarchs, notably of Henry III, was in due course to reduce the wealth of the Jewish financiers to a disastrous level, for the monarch was not always the most scrupulous repayer either of capital or of interest. (Part of this unhappy process was that the Jewish community provided funds, either as loans or by way of payment of fines levied on them, for Henry's enlargement of Westminster Abbey.) Henry's son Edward I completed the downfall of these early Jewish immigrants by commanding their expulsion from the country, and this ban was to remain in force for nearly four centuries.

Edward then turned for finance to other foreign residents in the City, this time to the merchants and in particular to the Lombards from northern Italy. In return for their assistance the king granted them certain privileges hitherto denied to foreigners by the City's own government, and this course of action precipitated a crisis in which the aldermen were once again enabled to affirm their right to elect a mayor of their choice rather then accept a nominee of the king, which had been their lot for some years past.

Nevertheless, the Lombards became established as financiers, and may be looked on as the real forerunners in England of much that goes on in banking as we know it today. It was they who introduced into Britain a system of bills of exchange and documents of credit for the financing of overseas trade. At a time when transport was slow and even a little un-certain, and the means of communication over long distances rudimentary (where they existed at all), it was essential for some form of binding obliga-tion to be recorded against which payment in coin could be made on delivery of the goods. It is from these financiers from cities such as Genoa, Venice and Florence that we derive much of the terminology used today in banking; even the word 'bank' itself may have originated with the Venetian financier's bench or *banco* in the market place.

The greater proportion by far of the business done by the Lombards was in respect of overseas trade generated by the navigators and merchants using the Port of London. Inland, matters were different and barter was freely used when cash was considered insufficient or even inappropriate. However, the accumulation of wealth both by merchants trading overseas

The Mint: aquatint by Pugin and Rowlandson

and, in time, by the agricultural community in the country made both the safe-keeping of that wealth and its transfer from hand to hand in the course of commerce a matter of importance. In London by the fourteenth and fifteenth centuries the goldsmiths performed both these functions. This was both natural and logical. As traders and workers in a metal that was both precious and in use as coin they possessed better than average safe-keeping facilities, and they were accustomed to handling both English and foreign money in quantity and to exchanging the one for the other when required.

The Royal Mint, which has only recently been moved out of the City, was until the mid seventeenth century another recognised safe-deposit for gold and coin. However, its reputation in this regard was rudely shaken when Charles I in 1640 actually took over deposits to the value of some £200,000 which had been placed at the Mint for safe-keeping. True, the money was in due course returned, but the episode did great harm to the Mint's standing as a safe-deposit, as well as confirming the reputation for financial irresponsibility of monarchs.

From the safe-keeping of wealth on behalf of its owners, and the exchange of one currency for another, the goldsmiths made further progress towards banking as we now think of it. They issued receipts for money deposited with them, and themselves paid interest to the depositors. Receipts passed from hand to hand as a convenient substitute for the physical transfer of the money or bullion itself and on the strength of these deposits the goldsmiths were able to lend a proportion to customers at a higher rate of interest than that which they were paying to the depositors. On the assumption that not all of the money deposited would be withdrawn at one time, it was quite prudent to make loans against a part of the total. Though the goldsmith's receipt for moneys or gold lodged was the true forerunner of the bank note, the extra refinement of issuing notes backed by other than specie was yet to come.

The goldsmiths also effected the transfer of specified amounts of customers' deposits on receipt of written instructions from the customers themselves, in order that they might make payment to other parties without the need to move their money from the goldsmith's keeping. Thus, along with the much older bill of exchange, were introduced both the bank note and the cheque.

But there remained one further development to be initiated by a rash or high-handed action on the part of the king. The goldsmiths themselves, after the Mint had fallen from grace in this respect, had been in the habit of depositing their own surplus funds for safe-keeping with the Exchequer, then situated in Tokenhouse Lane, behind Lothbury. King Charles II forced a loan from the Exchequer in 1672 in the vast sum of £1,300,000 to help finance the Dutch wars. Once again the City was faced with the severe problem of the security of its inhabitants' funds. This particular problem was exacerbated by an eighteen-year delay in payment of interest!

The concept of the City's own bank began to take shape in the minds of those whose wealth, or even livelihood, was from time to time jeopardised in this way. Eventually in 1693 William Paterson, a Scot, was spokesman before a committee of the House of Commons on behalf of a group who had conceived the idea of granting credit on a national scale on Parliamentary security through a City institution set up for this purpose. (This imaginative man is also remembered less happily for his part in raising the disastrous Scottish expedition to the swamps of Darien on the Panama Isthmus.) At this time William III, the Dutchman brought to the English throne in succession to the fugitive James II in 1688, was engaged in a war against France for the protection of his native Netherlands.

Finance on a large scale was required urgently. In 1694, primarily with the intention of raising the funds necessary for the conduct of the war, the Bank of England was founded and given a Royal Charter. The Bank's first loan was thus to the government and was in the sum of £1,200,000, to be repaid not before 1706 and to carry interest at the rate of £100,000 a year. So the Bank was, from its very beginnings, established as banker to the government though remaining a body independent of that government until the Bank of England Act 1946. (Even today, however, the 'Old Lady of Threadneedle Street' remains very much an individualist with an independent turn of mind.)

In its early days the Bank was content to operate a similar business to

The Great Hall of the Bank of England: aquatint by Pugin and Rowlandson

that of the goldsmiths, run along similar lines. It issued its own notes, as the goldsmiths were now doing, and so was not compelled to rely exclusively on the taking of deposits and lending against them for its income. It was this status as a bank of issue rather than solely as a bank of deposit which distinguished the young Bank of England from national banks in other countries. This difference was of some significance then, since it was not yet fully appreciated that it could conduct a viable business in its own right as a deposit bank; the issue of notes was at the time regarded as the more profitable part of a bank's business.

The Bank's Charter was renewed in 1708, and this time with a provision that the right to issue notes might not be extended to any body other than a partnership of fewer than six members (presumably to give the Bank a monopoly of note issue). This monopoly clause in the Charter was to influence the course of British banking in more than one way, but its most significant effect for our purpose here was virtually to prohibit any form of branch banking as we understand it today. In the City, the goldsmith bankers were for the most part unaffected, since the majority were either individuals or small partnerships. Elsewhere, the country banks found themselves unable to progress towards expansion of their activities. Furthermore, not being possessors of a deposit base wide enough to support such business, they were unable to grant loans of any great size. (Such restrictions did not apply in Scotland, which developed separately.)

The country banks had come into being owing to farmers and merchants in the provinces seeking to put their surplus funds to good use as had the goldsmiths in London. Their activities were connected with local markets and fairs, and their clientele and scope of operations were therefore comparatively local, with none of the foreign exchange and probably a smaller amount of deposit business than that enjoyed by the London bankers. However, they were able to assist their customers by discounting their bills of exchange. In turn, these bills could be rediscounted for cash in the London market and in such transactions the good standing of the banks themselves became of importance since such rediscounting would have been against their names.

This trade in inland bills led in the seventeenth century to the emergence of the bill broker as a distinct and separate feature in the entrepreneurial web now rapidly being woven. At first, they were content to put the holders of bills into contact with those who had spare cash with which to discount them, and to receive a commission for so doing. By the early nineteenth century certain of the bill brokers were coalescing into discount houses which carried bill portfolios themselves and financed their discounting by means of short-term borrowing from the banks in London. The Bank of England became then, and remains today, the lender of last resort to the discount market, which has itself expanded and developed its scope and business enormously, and yet remains unique – there is no comparable market elsewhere.

The importance of the discount houses today goes well beyond their original function as brokers of trade bills. Now they are at the centre of a large and intricate system for dealing with the short-term liquidity requirements of the banks and thus in effect balancing the books each day of the banking establishment itself. In so doing they act as the intermediaries between the banks and the Bank of England, to which they have direct access and from which they themselves may borrow overnight should it be necessary. It is not easy to convey in relatively few words exactly how these houses perform their function, but perhaps the best overall impression may be given by describing them as the City's own fine-tuning apparatus. This unique feature of London as a banking centre is the one which goes furthest towards providing the flexibility and the speed of operation of the entire mechanism. A very large and very rapid turnover makes small margins acceptable and the discount market is thus able to flourish whilst it provides a logistic service of the highest importance.

Whilst the Bank of England's monopoly position in the joint-stock banking field had been tolerable in its earlier years – and had indirectly been responsible for the beginnings of the discount market – changing conditions during and after the Industrial Revolution made it unworkable if not actually dangerous in terms of the security of the other, smaller banks. These were still restricted to partnerships with a set maximum of participants, since the Bank itself was as yet the only joint-stock institution in the field, with the benefit of shareholder participation and limited liability. With trade expanding enormously, so, too, did the burdens placed upon these banks and failures began to occur; in 1825 no fewer than 73 English banks stopped payment. (Scotland, which had enjoyed joint-stock banking from the outset, was largely spared these upheavals, though the failure of the City of Glasgow Bank in 1878 gave her own system a jolt.)

In 1826, therefore, the restriction as to the number of partners was lifted, and Parliament sanctioned the establishment of joint-stock banks, but not within 65 miles of London. Thus, the rearguard action fought by the supporters of the *status quo*, amongst whom were the London private banks, was not wholly unsuccessful.

For some years past, even the private banks in the City had found that the Bank of England notes were tending to overwhelm any opposition

An early nineteenth century bank note

in the field of note issue, and they had in consequence leaned more towards deposit banking, at which they found it possible to make quite acceptable profits. Accordingly, plans were put in train to test the Bank of England's monopoly by the establishment in London of a joint-stock deposit bank as distinct from a note-issuing bank. However, in 1833 the situation was resolved by the renewal of the Bank's Charter without any monopoly clause or other restriction on joint-stock banking nationwide.

In the matter of issuing notes, the Bank of England had established a dominant position by the second quarter of the nineteenth century, and the Charter Act 1833 made its notes legal tender. At this time it was still a matter of debate as to what proportion of a bank's notes in circulation ought to be backed by gold, and this applied particularly to those issued by the Bank of England. From the time of the goldsmiths, whose transferable receipts were the forerunners of the bank note, there had always been a school of thought which held that it was quite justifiable to issue notes in excess of the issuing bank's actual deposits of gold. Other securities were available as backing, and any sort of withdrawal of a heavy proportion of total deposits was regarded as unlikely. The matter appeared to have been resolved with the Charter Act 1844 which set a fixed limit to the amount of notes the Bank might issue against securities (the 'fiduciary issue' as it was known), whilst permitting flexibility in the number of notes in issue backed by gold.

An 1890s cheque and stub

Another effect of the Act was to reduce the number of notes in circulation issued by other joint-stock banks, since it forbade such issue by, *inter alia*, new combinations of banks resulting from mergers and amalgamations. In fact the last bank still to issue its own notes in England (the position was different north of the border) was Fox, Fowler & Company, which was absorbed by Lloyds Bank as recently as 1921.

However, in each of the financial crises which followed the Act of 1844 it was found necessary to suspend its provisions in this regard and to permit an increase in the fiduciary issue, and in 1914 at the outbreak of the First World War total flexibility became – and has remained – the order of the day.

The multiplicity of banks operating in London brought with it another and more immediately appreciable problem: the transfer of cheques from bank to bank and the receipt of cash in exchange. In the later seventeenth century the coffee houses were opening up, as the new beverage increased in popularity. Lloyd's, Jonathan's, the Jamaica, the Jerusalem, the Antwerp and others established for themselves a special position in the City as the recognised, though not always official, headquarters of many of its budding institutions. Of this we shall see more in later chapters.

It was not many years later that the banks' clerks in the course of their regular 'walks' through the City as messengers took to meeting in one or other of the coffee houses, the easier to exchange cheques. (Possibly, the due arrival at the correct bank of some of these cheques may have been somewhat at risk due to the then-prevailing degree of illiteracy even amongst what would now be called white-collar workers. London's street naming and the numbering of houses within streets has always been rather haphazard, and with these two factors in mind the banks were wont to display their badges prominently over their doors. Today, the tradition persists and these often beautiful coats of arms add a touch of colour and even splendour to the scene.)

From the first meetings for the exchange of cheques between clerks evolved the simple yet ingenious system of 'clearing': that is, of settling bank to bank only the difference remaining after exchange of cheques in bulk, rather than having to transfer possibly very large sums transaction by transaction. So in 1833 the Bankers' Clearing House came into being as a formalised organisation. This was in all probability the first clearing house as such, and it certainly predates the Commodity Clearing House by a wide margin. The Bankers' Clearing House was initiated by the private banks and it was not until 1854 that the 'new' joint-stock banks were admitted. With the development of the branch banking system by these new banks, the Clearing House became a real necessity; its turnover increased more than fivefold during the first thirty or so years of its existence and now stands at close on £2,000,000 millions worth of cheques passing through the clearings annually.

Along with the development of the branch banking system, the joint-stock banks, or 'new' banks as they were somewhat disparagingly called by their private contemporaries, were responsible for popularising and encouraging the banking habit amongst the population generally. Until the middle of the nineteenth century, the use of a bank and possession of a bank account were very much restricted to the wealthier class. Cheques at this time bore an *ad valorem* stamp duty, which greatly militated against their widespread use. The duty was reduced to one penny in 1853, was increased to twopence in 1918 and was not in fact done away with until 1971. However, with the duty on cheques reduced in 1853 it was far more attractive for smaller businessmen and for individuals to avail themselves of this simple facility, with the result that, for inland business at least, the bill of exchange was very much less used than before.

With the 'new' banking came the use of the overdraft. This was very soon seen as a more flexible and in many ways a simpler means of raising temporary finance than by the issue of bills and their subsequent acceptance and discounting. And it was in all probability the introduction and wide-spread use of this often misunderstood facility which did most to supersede the bill in inland trade. Later developments in hire purchase (originally conducted as a series of bills in respect of the instalments), personal loans with fixed repayments over a period, and the more recent bankers' credit cards have made inroads on the amount of pure overdraft business done, save for short-term 'tide-over' finance.

View of the **BANK** of **ENGLAND**, taken from the Corner of Bank Buildings.

This Elegant Building (in Front) was begun in 1771, by Sir Robt Taylor, & finished by him, 1783. The several additions that have since been made, was by He

Published 24.th June 1800 by LAURIE & WHITTLE, 53 Fleet Street London .

The Bank of England: an engraving of the building designed by Sir Robert Taylor

Though not strictly banking in the purest sense of the term, hire purchase deserves a mention here. It was initiated as a means of granting credit in respect of consumer durables shortly after the First World War, and made steady progress, notably in the financing of motor car sales. The original method of issuing a bill for each monthly instalment was largely superseded by an arrangement whereby the retailer sold the goods outright to the finance house, which in turn hired them to the customer, who finally bought them for a nominal sum after paying the equivalent of the purchase price plus interest by way of equal instalments. In fact, hire purchase, or something like it, had for many years past been the accepted method of purchasing, amongst other things, sewing machines, pianos and clothing via the 'Tallyman'.

Hire purchase has now largely been supplanted by various leasing and other arrangements in the field of commercial transport and capital equipment. In the consumer field the personal loan – in essence an overdraft reducing by regular repayments over an agreed period – and the credit card have made inroads on the original hire purchase method of raising credit. In offering finance in this way the banks and the finance houses look to the customer rather than to the goods as security: thus releasing themselves from what were often quite costly problems of repossession and resale of goods. The hire purchase houses have now almost all been absorbed by the clearing banks, who began to come into the field in the late 1950s.

Meanwhile the position of the Bank of England was undergoing change and development. From the early days of entrenched opposition to the setting-up of any other joint-stock bank, its attitude had altered markedly; when the Baring Brothers crisis arose in 1890 it was the Bank which organised the joint action (to the tune of some £17,500,000) necessary to retrieve the situation without any disastrous side-effects. In more recent times the Bank organised what is flippantly referred to as the 'Lifeboat' – special support by the collective action of some or all of the clearing banks – which rescued a number of financial institutions, both large and small, with severe liquidity problems due to their having been perhaps a shade impulsive in lending to developers against property, thus failing to observe banking's own basic maxim never to borrow short and lend long.

If the Bank of England is in any real sense the government's bank – and both its status and its relationship to the Treasury remain somewhat ill defined even after the 1946 Act which brought the Bank under the aegis of Parliament by a sort of nationalisation – it is also in a very real sense the City's bank. It maintains an attitude of constructiveness in considering new developments and projects as well as one almost of protectiveness in coping with some of Westminster's more alarming flights of fancy. That this situation could occur at all, still less be so smooth in operation, reflects much credit on the good sense of both the Bank itself and of the City institutions, all of whose daily activities impinge upon it and upon each other.

CHAPTER FOUR

Banking — The International Scene

We should now turn our attention to the provision of finance for trade other than the purely domestic, and see how the Port and the City between them have generated yet more business to be handled and managed from within the Square Mile.

Though its origins were contemporaneous with those of inland financing, and though both made the bill of exchange their original document, external banking activity was a later growth: it borrowed, and to a large degree adapted, some of the methods already in use for domestic business.

The importance of London as an international financial and banking centre became appreciable only after the seventeenth century, up to which time Antwerp, Amsterdam and other cities in turn had been dominant in this field. By the 1700s England's internal or domestic money market was a very highly developed one and by this time also – long periods of war notwithstanding – the amount of overseas trade passing through the Port of London had reached very large proportions. With these sure foundations to build upon, an international money market could be established which would attract funds from wherever there was a surplus seeking an investment outlet, as well as a longer-term capital market for the provision of funds for developing areas the world over. From the eighteenth century until 1914 and the outbreak of the First World War, London dominated the world's financial and banking scene with sterling universally respected and trusted – and backed by gold.

The development of joint-stock banking methods brought about a gradual decline in the use of the inland bill of exchange for the purpose of raising day-to-day finance. However, experience gained in this field was put to a profitable purpose in the accepting and discounting of bills on overseas customers. It was of course necessary for such bills to be accepted (in effect guaranteed) by somebody who was known to the London market as being of undoubted standing and yet who could feel the same confidence about the foreign drawer of the bill. In this field the merchant banks were pre-eminent. Themselves for the greater part derived or descended from trading houses, they each had their particular specialities; either in relation to the merchandise for which finance was required, or an intimate knowledge of the area whence those goods came or whither they were destined.

Many of the merchant banks owe their origin to the expansion of the activities of the merchants to include the acceptance of bills as well as trading on their own account. Trading either with their own or with chartered ships, they bought, sold and bartered goods in particular areas primarily for their own account. In so doing they were able to set up agencies or establish their own associates in those areas. From such a relationship it was but a step to act as banker for the overseas agent, who might leave his share of the proceeds of a sale in the hands of the merchant for the latter to invest in due course for him in London.

In time the merchant in London might also find himself in the position of accepting bills drawn by houses other than his own immediate agent or connection in the foreign country of export. When the figures for export and for import did not match, then the need was created for a truly inter-

The Port of London: print by T. Allom

national movement of credit. The occasions in early days when this imbalance occurred were not infrequent, since export and import trades tended to be operated separately. This division was usually the outcome of restrictions imposed locally on who might or might not be permitted to use a particular port or ply in a particular product. Later, as two-way trade became more usual and more easily effected, it became a question of balancing the import/export books in terms of money and later still in terms of the marketability of money in various denominations. Such movement of credit was often in respect of third-country trade, where the goods in question never reached these shores at all.

The early merchant venturers were by no means all natives of these islands. (Amongst the earliest names associated with sailing out of British ports, Cabot for example was of Venetian stock.) However, names of many Englishmen, such as Frobisher and Hawkins, spring to mind and serve to demonstrate that Britain also possessed her quota. In the context of later development into merchant banks it proved to be the venturers from the ports of continental Europe who were of greater significance. Venetians – such as Marco Polo who opened the Silk Route to Cathay and the Far East – Hansards from the Baltic and North German ports, Gascons in the wine trade from French Biscay and the Dutch from the Rhine Delta were all active. All had their particular sphere of operations and all evolved their individual expertise.

It was for the most part from these men and their descendants that the great merchant banking names are drawn: Hambro, Lazard, Schroder to name but a few. London's reputation as an international trade and banking centre drew such families to these shores, all too frequently the transplantation having been hastened by political or religious intolerance in their own native countries. Warburg, for example, came here following the exodus from Hitler's Germany. It was therefore probably inevitable that most of the merchant banking houses should have been established by, and carry the names of these *emigrés* from other lands. Britain was a country where not many impediments existed in the way of settling and setting-up in business. Today it is the banks with origins from overseas which form the majority in the list of merchant banks and relatively few, such as Antony Gibbs and Arbuthnot Latham represent those of native origin.

It is as well at this point to attempt a definition of the term 'merchant bank', since we shall be encountering them in two different contexts. It is a curious fact that in the United Kingdom there exists no precise legal definition of a bank as such: legislation has from time to time produced more or less lucid criteria for identifying various parts of the mysterious whole which makes up a bank, but no more. It is also rather unfortunate that a number of institutions, whose business undoubtedly included the receiving and the lending of money, chose, in recent years, to describe themselves rather precociously as merchant banks. These 'fringe banks' or, more politely, secondary banks have had their day; some are still languishing in the Bank of England 'lifeboat' (whereby the clearing banks under Bank of England coordination provided funds in the more extreme cases of illiquidity resulting from over-enthusiastic lending) whilst others have sunk without trace. What then is a merchant bank?

Perhaps the easiest definition is that applied by the merchant banks themselves in their admissions to either or both of two bodies representing their main activities today. One of these is the Issuing Houses Association, of which we shall see more when we consider the Stock Exchange and the capital market. The other and smaller of the two is the Accepting Houses Committee whose members, in the words of the report of the Radcliffe Committee on the Workings of the Monetary System (1959), 'are nearly all companies, including some public companies, but all of them retaining a strong element of their traditional ownership and management by families, some of whose names have stood high in world finance for a century or more'. These are the accepting houses which are of immediate relevance to us at this point.

The Accepting Houses Committee came into being at the outbreak of the First World War. As may be imagined, a major liquidity problem faced many of the merchant banks which had accounts open with now-hostile nations, and which of course were left unpaid. It was urgently necessary to afford financial assistance where it was needed, and to do so in close consultation with the Bank of England and the government of the day. After the armistice in 1918 it was felt by all concerned that the Committee should stay in being, partly as a forum for discussion amongst its own members and partly as a link between them and the government and other authorities whereby they might all speak with one voice. The Committee has no rigid nor formal rules, though it does have a Director General and a small headquarters staff. When Britain joined the European Economic Community in 1972, the Committee was incorporated into the British Bankers' Association and is thus officially a participant in that body's dealings with the EEC Commission.

Thus the increasing business of overseas and international finance by way of the bill on London was facilitated by the emergence of certain of the merchant banks as accepting houses who added their own names to bills and so made them the more readily and cheaply transferable in the market. By accepting a bill in this way the merchant bank put itself in the position of payer, so far as the lending bank was concerned, and the latter was then in a better position to provide the finance with less risk and consequently at a finer rate.

As the discount houses developed and improved bill broking into a whole, distinct and vital market in short-term credit, so the accepting houses henceforward were to build on the foundation of lending their name to the bills of those known to or connected with them and transform this into a business in its own right and of great importance to international trade. In terms of their influence and importance in this regard the heyday of the merchant banks came during and immediately after the Napoleonic Wars, when they were responsible for raising very large funds for the British Government. In later years they were to perform the same service for many governments overseas, as country after country found in the nineteenth century that its external trade was expanding and that as a consequence its own internal liquidity was coming under strain.

So third-country financing became a major part of the activity of the City. With the then unrivalled status of sterling, it was often considered preferable by foreign traders to settle business with each other in sterling in London by way of the bill on London, rather than in local currencies with attendant mutual exchange problems. It was not long before the merchant banks found themselves holders of deposits on behalf of overseas governments also, as the settlement of business in sterling began to find favour in their eyes as well as in those of the commercial sectors amongst their nationals.

London in the nineteenth century became the almost universal provider of development and other finance the world over, and the centre for handling transactions in the one currency in which at the time vitually all international obligations were discharged. History has changed this particular aspect of things, though the standing of the City remains unimpaired despite the decline in the international prestige of sterling, this being largely due to the City's already acquired expertise in dealings in other currencies and in other directions. Such experience, gained over many years, is not rapidly or readily exportable and this fact goes some way towards accounting for the inflow of foreign banks to London – of which we shall see more in Chapter 9.

One effect of the dominant position of sterling in international transactions

The Royal Exchange: an engraving on the invitation for the laying of the foundation stone in 1842

Admit the Bearer

To witness the Ceremony of laying

THE

FIRST STONE

OF THE

NEW ROYAL EXCHANGE,

on Monday the 17th January, 1842.

James Barnes

THE ENTRANCE IS FROM CORNHILL, AND THE TIME OF ADMISSION WILL BE, NOT EARLIER THAN
12, NOR LATER THAN **2** O'CLOCK.

Nº 1059

up to 1914 was the relatively late development of the foreign exchange market in London. For so long as this situation persisted it was clearly more important for centres other than London to occupy themselves in the exchange of sterling into local currencies as local conditions demanded, and then to trade those currencies against each other. It was also possible to convert sterling easily into gold and thus immediately to establish its international exchange value.

It may be assumed that early forays into the business of foreign exchange were carried out by the physical weighing of the coin for its value as metal. Progress towards the exchange of money at a fixed or floating rate was, however, faster than one might have imagined; it appears that transactions of this nature were being done at least as early in history as the Roman occupation of Britain. But the concept of some form of organised market in foreign exchange on an international level is of much more recent origin; even today it has to be admitted that unilateral shifts in rates as a matter of temporary political expediency occasionally upset what ought to be re-garded as the correct function of an exchange system. Such, sometimes arbitrary, alterations in the international value of a currency, whether by outright devaluation or revaluation or by the more subtle means of 'inter-vention' in the market by a central bank, can also cause a distortion in the forward value of the currency assessed by the market as a factor of anticipated supply and demand considerations in much the same way as is done with commodities. After all, money is a commodity and its various denominations move in and out of fashion rather as do physical commodities of different origin and purity.

Until the First World War the merchant banks used to meet daily in the Royal Exchange with the representatives of those overseas banks which were then established in London. Though this procedure ceased with the outbreak of war, and was not in fact reinstated after the cessation of hostilities, a comparable practice is still observed in many other European centres.

Today the foreign exchange market in London has no headquarters as such nor any central assembly point. Like many other activities in the City, foreign exchange business is carried on by individual specialists, known collectively as 'the Market'. In world terms the communications centre is still London, with London prices and rates an essential point of reference though other markets in other cities are by now of equal or greater im-portance in connection with one or other particular aspect of foreign exchange dealing. This may apply notably in arbitrage, where a bank may buy money in one centre and sell it in another, taking advantage of a difference in the relative exchange rates, depending all the time on a variety of factors, amongst which the freedom to buy or to deliver a currency may be affected by local legislation.

Between the two world wars, London's development as an important and influential market in foreign exchange was rapid. This was once again due to traditional financial expertise, but there was in addition a matter of simple geography. As communications became more rapid and more efficient, with the increase in the use of international cable and telephone links, and later with the introduction of telex, London's happy situation upon longitude zero (at the centre of the world's time zones) was turned to her advantage.

During the inter-war period (aside from a short time between 1925 and 1931) Britain was no longer on the gold standard. Sterling was in consequence no longer freely transferable into gold, and so became less stable and less readily valued. As an inevitable result, more and more imports were invoiced in other currencies, and the need for a sophisticated foreign exchange market became more strongly felt, to the extent that the clearing banks themselves opened their own dealing rooms and operated alongside the merchant banks and the foreign banks then in London.

Banks conduct their foreign exchange business in their own name as principals. Thus there was room for a whole sector of foreign exchange brokers to come into the picture, whose function is to match sellers with buyers and for so doing they receive a commission. After the end of the last war these brokers formed themselves into an association (Foreign Exchange and Currency Deposit Brokers Association) – initially with eight members – so as to bring a little more order into the market. This association works with, but remains independent of, a comparable body, the Foreign Exchange Committee (now part of the British Bankers Association), which had been set up by the clearing banks shortly before the war.

After Britain finally left the gold standard in 1931 there followed once more a period of floating exchange rates. But this time the floating of sterling was to an extent controlled in two ways. The first was the existence of the Exchange Equalisation Account, which was set up in order to support the rate in dealings on overseas markets and so to maintain it as close as possible to the official rate. The second inhibiting factor was the Tripartite Agreement between the United Kingdom, the United States and France. On the outbreak of war the belligerents once more pegged their exchange rates, and such dealings as there were had to be done through the respective central banks. So the markets in Europe were closed until after the cessation of hostilities, and even then business in foreign exchange was heavily restricted for an appreciable time.

The foreign exchange market in London was reopened in 1951, though dealings were still hedged about with restrictions. It was not for some years that the London market was able to resume anything like its old pre-eminence. Sterling itself had lost, and has so far shown no real sign of regaining, its erstwhile position of favour as a trading currency in the international sense. As a reserve asset it has been superseded by the US dollar, though the 'mighty dollar', too, has in recent years shown alarming symptoms of weakness. It seems most unlikely that we shall again see any one currency remaining in favour and holding its value in anything like the way sterling did in the conditions obtaining in its heyday, because it is most unlikely that we shall ever witness a repeat of those conditions.

Dealings in bullion, and the London markets in gold, silver and platinum are in many ways difficult to place in their correct context: these markets have many characteristics in common with both banking and commodity trading. However, the close connection of the merchant banks with the bullion markets prompts their inclusion here, and a kind of parallel may be drawn with foreign exchange dealings. Although being a physical entity, bullion may be delivered in any location, and premiums or discounts in local prices over or beneath the officially quoted market price reflect local supply and demand conditions.

In the cases of gold and of silver, trading in London has a history as long as that of the City itself with its origins in the actual transfer of coin or tokens in exchange for merchandise. The separation of this direct business from the more abstract commerce of dealing in bars of a standard weight and purity was a gradual affair. For the record, Mocatta & Goldsmid (which became a part of the Hambro's merchant banking group in 1957) was founded in 1684, and since 1696 has been the silver broker for the Bank of England.

The London Silver Market in its present form may be said to have originated in the 1880s, when Mocatta & Goldsmid, Pixley & Abell and Sharps & Wilkins – all of whom had for many years been trading in precious metals – started a weekly silver 'fixing'. A fixing may be defined as the arriving at a base price, founded on supply and demand, which may then be used as a reference for dealings both spot and forward until the next 'fix'. The daily silver fixing was instituted at the beginning of the present century and now takes place at 12.15 each working day. Samuel Montagu joined the Silver Market in 1900, and the two other original members, aside from Mocatta, merged to form Sharps, Pixley which was itself absorbed into the Kleinwort Benson group in 1963. With the earlier absorption by Hambros of Mocatta & Goldsmid, and the arrival on the market of N. M. Rothschild the connection with the accepting houses became even closer.

All these companies, along with Johnson Matthey Bankers Ltd (who are also members of the Silver Market) comprise the Bullion Market where Rothschilds take the chair at the daily gold fixing. Whilst dealing in gold, save in the form of coin or of medals, remains outside the purview of the investor in Britain, it is possible for him to operate in silver and platinum, and there is frequently quite a lively arbitrage between silver on the Metal Exchange and on the London Silver Market.

There have been other developments connected with, or consequent

A gold fixing taking place at Rothschilds

upon, the post-war shift in political and economic emphasis which on balance have been fortunate for London as an international banking centre. One of these is the emergence in a new guise of the British overseas banks. These are the houses which were formed with their headquarters in London but whose function was to provide a banking service in the territories of the Empire. Originally they were what are termed retail banks, offering a service direct to customers 'over the counter'. As the various territories have gained their independence as sovereign states in their own right, the overseas banks have undergone certain changes in structure and in emphasis. The newly-independent countries quite naturally did not wish to see a large proportion of their national resources in terms of finance controlled from elsewhere. In order therefore to accommodate their wishes these banks have tended to set up local offshoots with the government of the particular country or with other local investors taking up a majority in their shares, or at least a significant minority interest.

The overseas banks meanwhile have added to their traditional retail facilities the further activities of wholesale, corporate and offshore banking. In this way old links have been maintained and yet another strand in the web of London's financial ramifications spun.

An attempt at a short chapter on the international banking aspect of the City must unavoidably omit almost as much as it includes. This is in the main due to the connection between international banking and the whole structure of international politics and economics. A very great deal of what happens is but a part of a wide-reaching process in the political sphere, to which any more specialised machinery must be subject – in terms not necessarily of what it does but of how it is permitted to operate and where it should look for opportunity. Through all this somewhat muddled development, however, there stands out clearly the continuous thread of the bill on London, introduced and promoted into general use by the commercially gifted Lombards, and whose scope of employment has been expanded by successive generations of merchant bankers and by the discount houses. The inland bill was first given legal sanction by an Act of 1697, and the entire system of trading through bills of exchange in England was definitively codified in the Bills of Exchange Act 1882, which still governs their use.

In sum, we may say that if the banking system centred on the City appears today to be a far cry from that first tentatively introduced by the goldsmiths, there remain many features which the latter would recognise, as well as others of which they might have said 'given a little more time, and we would have done it'. Progress may have been patchy but it has nonetheless been impressive. The fact that no fewer than 48 per cent of the adult population of these islands have current accounts with a bank is a measure of the progress made in bringing retail banking to the public. (The growth of the use of current accounts has not been steady and the last big increase was after the introduction of bankers cards.) In terms of the finance of trade the picture is as clear. Without the advantage of a dominant currency the banking sector has more than maintained its position since the Second World War. Meanwhile, in terms of traditional banking and of the manifold peripheral services that today go along with it, first and foremost among the forces and influences which have fostered its progress in the service of trade and the movement of goods must rank the bill of exchange.

CHAPTER FIVE

The Commodity Markets

Commodity trading in London takes three distinct forms which, though they interact upon each other (and none would be so important or so active without the others), they are nevertheless quite different in purpose. Of these interfaces, the first to emerge was the direct import and export of essential raw materials. The second is a business, or more properly a collection of separate businesses which had its origins in direct import and export but which developed into an almost world-wide third country or entrepôt trade. And the third is the commodity terminal market as we know it today.

We have already taken a look at the direct business of the movement of goods, and in later chapters we shall read something of the ancillary, yet essential, financial and insurance services which accompany such dealings. Let us look now, therefore, at the two other aspects of commodity trading – merchanting, or third country trade, and the terminal market dealing in obligations to take or make delivery.

Each of these is dependent upon the use of credit and the instruments of credit (indeed futures trading could not exist without credit). It is also true to say that terminal market trading owes much of its present-day efficacy to the revolution in communications brought about by the invention of the telegraph.

Before the widespread use of more or less instantaneous communication over great distances, it was vital for merchants and others concerned in a particular trade to meet and exchange information direct. Only with the transmission of reasonably up-to-date news does it become possible for an idea of prices and deliveries to crystallise sufficiently for business actually to be done. It is interesting and amusing to observe just how necessary

Sir Thomas Gresham

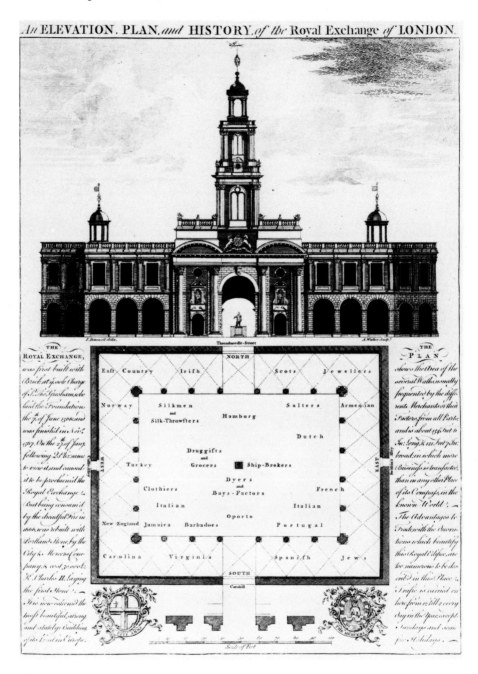

A plan of the second Royal Exchange

this facility for direct contact face to face is considered even today, when every office is connected with the rest of the world by telephone and telex – not to mention the ubiquitous visual display unit. Commodity brokers and merchants still find occasion to meet, and there are in the City today a number of twentieth century counterparts of the eighteenth century coffee houses, where 'shop' is talked at all levels over a cup or glass.

Before we consider the coffee houses we should spare a thought for Sir Thomas Gresham's Royal Exchange where today's commodity markets had their origins. This was conceived and constructed to provide in London an equivalent of the bourses already established in Continental centres such as Antwerp. Opened by Queen Elizabeth I in 1571, the Exchange was twice destroyed by fire – first in the Great Fire of 1666 and again in the early nineteenth century. The present building was opened by Queen Victoria in 1844 and only relinquished its last commercial use when Lloyd's moved from there in 1928. The building contained various 'walks' where those concerned with a particular trade foregathered at certain regular times to exchange information and to do business, but by the later eighteenth century and after the great expansion of international trade handled and financed in London, the Royal Exchange was no longer adequate to fulfil its original function.

The coffee houses, which began opening up in the City with the increasing popularity of the new beverage from the Levant, proved both convenient and congenial places for merchants to meet. Merchants tended to gravitate towards particular houses where members of one or possibly a few trades, or those dealing with a particular locality, would form the major part of the proprietor's clientele. Some of the landlords even made a point of having up-to-date news and advertisements and the like prominently on display. Jonathan's, the Jerusalem, the Virginia, Garraway's and Lloyd's are perhaps the most famous names; housing the embryos of what were to become such respected institutions as the Stock Exchange, the Baltic, the Metal Exchange and Lloyd's of London. Of the most readily identifiable survivors the Jamaica Inn in St Michael's Alley is perhaps the best known.

At this point perhaps we should consider the basic documentation by which it is possible to transfer title to very valuable parcels of goods in an open market 'on the nod'. The dock warrant was essential to the legal and indisputable transfer of title to goods bought and sold on a 'sight unseen' basis. The warrant was certainly in use in the first quarter of the eighteenth century in connection with sales by the East India Company and, with the ensuing expansion of the sale of 'goods in warehouse', it rapidly achieved widespread use as a document of title transferable by endorsement. This made possible change of ownership without any actual movement of the goods in question. The warrant, like the bill of lading, was suitable paper for offering as collateral against bank finance, and today the banks and merchant banks play a most important part in the financing of goods in warehouse and so afford a measure of liquidity to those dealing in the markets.

Title to merchandise could thus change hands direct between principals by the simple transfer of warrants, and as time went on merchants trading either for themselves, or as agent for either party to a contract, emerged as a very necessary factor in facilitating the movement of commodities from producers in one country to consumers in another. This, of course, was without actually handling or even seeing the goods in question.

However, the merchants needed a recognised forum where prices could be arrived at in public on the basis of world-wide supply and demand and, equally important, where they might cover their financial risk by 'hedging' on the market. At the outset goods were bought and sold on the basis of dock warrants, covering merchandise already landed and available for inspection and transfer. The next stage to develop, greatly assisted by improving communications, was the offering for sale of goods 'on arrival of ship'. These goods might either already be at sea *en route* for a stated destination, or they could still be awaiting embarkation from a port in the producing country. Either way, they were tangibly in existence at the time the offer was made. Such offers for sale on arrival were a convenient method whereby the producer could ensure a price before the commencement of the voyage, which could well be lengthy and the whole market picture might alter during the course of it – to the detriment of the producer.

The final stage of trading in 'futures', or in promises to make or take delivery on a future date without the actual possession by the seller of documents to an existing parcel, was a natural step. One of the earliest examples of futures trading pure and simple was the speculation which took place in the Amsterdam markets during the eighteenth century. The first instance in London of a departure from straightforward dealing in specific goods covered by specific documents was the 'general warrant' in Scottish pig iron which was introduced in the mid nineteenth century. This was a most important development since it introduced the concept of trading in perfectly standard goods, thus obviating the need for any bargaining over the quality or weight of any particular parcel. Though it has been many years since pig iron was traded on a London market, the practice of

Warehousing: a print by Gustav Doré

trading in standard lots of a set quality (within the permissible variation laid down) completed the framework of the modern commodity terminal market.

The increase in turnover and importance of what are sometimes rather unfairly dubbed 'paper markets' at the expense of auctions and sales of actual goods was in large measure due to two influences. In the first place changing techniques in cargo handling and increasing off-quay transport congestion led to a wider dispersal of cargoes to other ports. Secondly, the whole pattern of international trade has altered since the Second World War and there is now a much higher proportion of direct transport from producer to consumer. Thus the importance of the London warehouses as centres for distribution has been reduced and so has the number of produce auctions regularly held in London. Today these are relatively few, amongst which are the auctions and sales of tea, furs and ivory.

The origins of almost all the London commodity markets in their present form lie in the latter part of the nineteenth century. The markets have in the main followed one of three principal lines of development. The largest group – those embracing what are known as the 'soft commodities', i.e. foodstuffs for the most part – established itself after the coffee house era in the London Commercial Sale Rooms in Mincing Lane. (Though they are now housed one street further east, in Mark Lane, they are still collectively referred to as the Mincing Lane Markets.)

The original Commercial Sale Rooms were reconstructed and enlarged in 1890, and for the first time they were incorporated as a public company (capitalised with 1647 shares of £10 each plus a further £120,000 of debentures). There were some 1500 subscribers, and only they or their authorised representatives were permitted entry to the Subscription Room where commodity sales under the rules of the various commodity market associations were conducted. Then, as now, the markets were conducted on the open outcry principle, with bids and offers being called across the floor, giving an appearance to the stranger of total confusion.

The Commercial Sale Rooms building was destroyed by bombs in 1941 and members were compelled to transfer their operations. They went to Plantation House, a large and labyrinthine building occupying a site bounded by Eastcheap, Rood Lane, Fenchurch Street and Mincing Lane. It was built between the wars with, as its name implies, the commodity trade in mind. The Rubber Exchange was already in residence in Plantation House, and the other markets all foregathered to trade in the Rubber Market room. In 1954 a new company came into being – the London Commodity Exchange Company Ltd.

The LCE is so organised that although it has its own board of directors and floor committee, the actual running of the several markets remains in the hands of their own respective associations under their own committees of management and with their own supporting staff. Recently the LCE itself moved into the Corn Exchange building in Mark Lane, and the soft commodity markets now enjoy relatively commodious accommodation there, with excellent facilities. However, a proposal is now afoot to house all the markets (including the Baltic and the Metal Exchange) under one roof. To date this is but an idea for discussion and no actual moves are immediately likely.

The London Metal Exchange evolved quite independently from the corpus of the soft commodity markets and it operates on a quite different basis, without any centralised clearing of its members' contracts. Though all are under the same aegis and combine within one market organisation there are in fact seven markets in non-ferrous metals on the LME – in copper, lead, tin, silver, zinc, aluminium and nickel (the last two .of which were introduced in 1978 and 1979 respectively).

The metal merchants are recorded as having met regularly in one of the walks of the Royal Exchange, then in the Jerusalem coffee house and from 1869 in the then recently established Lombard Exchange and News Room in Lombard Court. The Exchange first appeared as a formal entity in 1876 when the London Metal Exchange Company was incorporated with a capital of £1500.

In 1882 the premises were considered too cramped and a new home for the market was found in Whittington Avenue by the Leadenhall Market, where the LME still resides. At the same time a new company was formed – the Metal Market & Exchange Company Ltd – and this company, along with a committee of subscribers, controls the exchange in a rather unique two-headed manner.

As with metals, so with grain. With the coming of the Industrial Revolution, Britain found herself a net importer of corn, and it became necessary to set up a market for trading and pricing incoming shipments. The Corn Exchange in London had long been in existence when the 'New' Exchange was opened in 1828 in Mark Lane. This market dealt in sales of corn discharged from ships in the London Docks. The sales were by sample and it was not concerned with anything other than direct physical trading. However, another London market in grain, and one which made the transition through arrivals to futures trading, was that first conducted in the Baltic coffee house. Here, both third country onward trade and direct imports to Britain were negotiated by professional market men – brokers

The Ring at the London Metal Exchange

and dealers. This was a well-organised market even in the early years of the nineteenth century. Its first committee met in 1823 when a set of formal rules was devised.

The position of the Baltic in the grain trade derives from the dominance of imports from northern Europe – especially from Russia – before imports from America commenced, and it is quite logical therefore that the terminal market in grain should from its early days have had its home there. With the relative speed and efficiency of communications overland from the grain exporting centres bordering the Black Sea and with Constantinople as a sort of nerve-centre, the trade in arrivals was developed to a high degree.

With an efficient forward market trading in arrivals, who needs futures?

It is a fact of life, however – whatever one's opinion of the futures market with its admitted scope for dealings based on purely financial considerations – that the trade in any given article can be subject to extreme price fluctuations, which a futures market can go a long way towards reducing. Thus it was with grain in the nineteenth century. The Napoleonic wars and later the war in the Crimea caused huge disturbances in supply, whose effect on prices in Britain a series of enactments over the period had failed to mitigate. It became clear to those close to the market that a hedging facility would be very desirable.

Futures trading in grain actually developed first across the Atlantic in the Chicago Board of Trade. In Britain, Liverpool was ahead of London in trading futures, as this way a natural extension of the trade in arrivals between that port and ports in the United States after the development of the wheatlands of the Middle West.

The London Corn Trade Association was set up in 1878 and incorporated as a company in 1886, remaining a separate entity from the Baltic itself. The first futures contract in grain in the United Kingdom was introduced in 1887 but it was not successful. This was mainly because adequate standardisation was not even attempted. A couple of years later successful contracts were launched in wheat and in maize (corn). Both were, however, doomed to a fairly short life, and in 1897 a new contract based on Northern Spring No. 1 wheat was launched. This was significant in that it introduced the Chicago practice of parcelling by weight rather than by volume.

Both London and Liverpool markets were closed for trading during the First World War, and though Liverpool reopened in 1921 the London futures market was not opened again until 1929. In the same year the two London markets merged to form the new London Corn Exchange, though later they once again went their separate ways. Today the Corn Exchange continues to be active in dealings in actuals, where samples are tendered, and is patronised by some two thousand members, many of whom have their market offices in the building in Mark Lane. It is said, by the way, that the stranger can always tell when there is a sale in progress by the number of pigeons foregathered in Mark Lane to gather up the samples after they have been discarded by the traders. During the Second World War both London and Liverpool were again closed and both suffered from bombing, with premises and a number of storage warehouses being damaged or lost.

The London Grain Futures Association was formed from amongst existing members of the Corn Trade Association in order to manage the futures market there, and in 1971 the Association amalgamated with the

Cattle Food Trade Association to form the Grain and Feed Trades Association (GAFTA) as we know it today. GAFTA has its headquarters in the same building as the Baltic, and the ring of the grain futures market is situated on a part of the floor of the Baltic Exchange. However, the two organisations remain independent of each other as regards management and membership. In addition to trading wheat and barley (the latter now based on an EEC standard) GAFTA introduced a successful market in soya bean meal in April 1975.

It is not easy to pin down precisely the date at which the earliest dealings in coffee took place in London, although we do know that the beverage was introduced (originally from Turkey) in the seventeenth century and rapidly became very fashionable. The coffee house indeed was the ideal social and business refuge for those to whom the ale houses were becoming progressively less attractive. An advertisement handbill of the period also went so far as to claim that coffee was both a preventive and a cure for such diverse ailments as dropsy, scurvy and gout. It was not until after the Napoleonic wars that Britain came to possess the major European coffee market when London succeeded Le Havre which had earlier succeeded Amsterdam. A high proportion of dealings in London were in respect of coffee destined for re-export and it was largely to the already established expertise in financing and handling entrepôt trade that the market in London owed its success.

The coffee terminal market in London dates from 1888, when a futures exchange was set up via the Coffee Trade Association, with its contracts cleared and guaranteed by the infant London Produce Clearing House (see page 71). The original contract was based on Brazilian No. 5 Santos coffee, though today Robusta constitutes the main contractual grade.

Meanwhile with sugar the picture was different in detail but not in broad principle. Crops grown on an annual basis can be, and from time to time are, subject to variations in supply such as are hardly known to the 'man-produced' or mined minerals and hydrocarbons. Initially the West Indies were the main source of cane sugar and, though it had been imported for many years previously, sugar had come to constitute one of the United Kingdom's most important inward markets by the early nineteenth century. It almost gained a strategic significance during the blockade of the Continent in the wars against France, and legend has it that illicit supplies were carried dressed into ladies' hair and men's wigs!

The terminal market in sugar was instituted with the incorporation of the first Sugar Exchange in Hamburg in 1880. A London market followed in 1888, based at first on the Hamburg contract – an indication of Britain's increasing dependence on imports of European beet sugar. Both markets closed during the First World War, though London reopened in 1921, based this time on an 'in-warehouse' London contract. Sugar, too, was beset between the wars with price stabilisation exercises of the kind which afflicted markets in other essential commodities; in particular owing to the quantities of sugar produced by countries within the Empire and the Commonwealth where attempts were made at securing some form of preferential treatment. After the end of World War II there was some delay in returning to free-market conditions, and it was not until 1957 that trading in sugar recommenced under the aegis of the United Terminal Sugar Market Association.

Cocoa as a beverage has a long history, and there is a rather nice comment in one of Samuel Pepys' diaries concerning a visit to a coffee house to 'drink jocolatte – very good'. The crop originated in the Amazon and Orinoco basins and was regarded by the inhabitants as possessing magic qualities, which caused it to be treated with a measure of caution by the early European explorers – a far cry from its rather mundane image today!

Futures trading in cocoa did not come until after the First World War, at first with the opening of a market in New York in 1925, and later (1928) in London; the Cocoa Association of London having been formed in 1926. Originally, trading in London took place on part of the floor of the Rubber Exchange in No. 7 Mincing Lane. After the Second World War the exchange was reopened relatively early, as cocoa was largely a sterling commodity and in consequence there were no serious foreign exchange problems. This time the market came under the authority of the London Cocoa Terminal Market Association.

Rubber must surely rank as one of the growth stories of the age. From a world production of natural rubber of only about 70,000 tons at the turn of the century, the figure has increased to some two and a half million tons. Add to this the development of synthetic rubber, whose production exceeds that of natural, and the fact that the latter is a commodity with a comparatively long growth cycle, and it can be seen that marketing rubber has its own special problems. At first, imported rubber was disposed of by auction in Liverpool and in the Commercial Sale Rooms in London. Other European markets existed in various centres, including Lisbon, where imports from the Portuguese Empire were traded. In 1907 a Rubber Growers' Association was founded, and the Rubber Trade Association of London came into being in 1913 to regulate the fortnightly auctions.

Forward sales had been going on in a limited way since the 1890s, and in 1921 the RTA drew up a set of regulations for the conduct of the market, formalising the contracts and fixing standards based on permanent type-samples. Also in 1921 the Rubber Settlement House was set up to register all forward contracts, which extend further into the future than those on the other markets. Settlements were made twice monthly on the basis of official prices, set each alternate Tuesday; in this way significantly reducing the risk of a major loss, with attendant embarrassment to all, at the end of what might be a very long futures contract. Today the contracts are cleared by the International Commodities Clearing House – formerly the London Produce Clearing House – which merits our attention as being in many ways the key to the success of the London markets.

The Sale Room at India House: aquatint by Pugin and Rowlandson

In 1888 a group of financiers, which included many prominent amongst the merchant banks, combined to fund the establishment of the London Produce Clearing House. To quote from the original Articles: 'The object of the Company is to place on a secure basis, by a system of deposits, the dealing in produce for future delivery, which has become such an important development both in Europe and in America.' Such an institution already existed in Le Havre (*la Caisse de Liquidation*) and in Hamburg. The latter was selected as the example to be followed and for some years Germans held senior positions in the staff of the LPCH.

The flotation was comfortably over-subscribed, and the company commenced with the clearing of contracts in sugar and coffee, with wheat and maize added one year later. Maize attracted little attention and at first the wheat contract was not a success – it revived somewhat in the late 1890s, but ceased in 1905 after the great wheat rust epidemic. (Wheat contracts are in fact now cleared once more.)

The LPCH was closed down during the Second World War, and was in real risk of being wound up. However in 1950 after a long period of inactivity its entire equity was purchased by United Dominions Trust Ltd, a finance house seeking both diversification and expansion. The purchaser made it a condition that the merchant bankers Antony Gibbs & Sons remain as secretaries to, and managers of the Clearing House, and this proved to be a most happy relationship for many years during which the LPCH was revitalised. Pioneering included a new futures market in copra in the 1950s (which was not continued) and in wool tops in 1953. The establishment of the latter was something of a saga, bringing as it did the voice of the Bradford wool industry into what was at times quite a hot debate – not everybody welcomes a terminal market in his trade when it is first mooted. The International Commodities Clearing House, as it is now styled, has its own computerised recording, registration and contracts clearing system and it is worth noting that this produces the very welcome spin-off of a really comprehensive statistical service to the markets it covers.

What does it do? In brief, the Clearing House registers all contracts done on the markets it serves, calling for an initial deposit from the parties. As the contracts proceed towards maturity, further sums by way of margin will be called from the party against whom the price may be moving (seller in a rising market and buyer in a falling one) in order that each one's stake in the contract matches its value at any time. Furthermore, in registering the contracts the Clearing House (which is an independent entity) guarantees their fulfilment at maturity. This is achieved by the process of substituting another party by 'novation' should either of the original contractors fall out. Perhaps the most important outcome of this novation process is that at any time a party may terminate a futures contract by executing an opposite one for the same date and tonnage. The two cancel each other out, leaving only a cash difference in relative prices to be accounted for and this too will be comparatively minor as margins will have been called and paid in the meantime. This facility for 'washing out' without the need to wait until the maturity date gives the markets an enormous flexibility.

The Baltic originated as yet another group of men with common interests meeting in one of the coffee houses to exchange news and to do business. First meetings were held in the Virginia and Maryland (a name redolent of other areas of trade) and such was the influence of this clientele with its interests in northern Europe and Russia that the coffee house itself changed its name to the Virginia and Baltic in 1744. Later, in 1810, these same trading houses shifted their meeting place to the Antwerp in Threadneedle Street, which was promptly restyled the Baltic Coffee House. Later still the organisation, for such it had now become, moved its headquarters to South Sea House.

Many of the merchants trading on the Baltic in the early days were of Greek origin. These Greek merchants had come to England for the most part in the eighteenth century, acting as the agents here for the producers in the Levant, and in due time they were conducting much of the London end of the Russian grain trade on their own account. This, combined with the relative ease and rapidity of communications from Constantinople, led to the early introduction of arrivals dealings in the market, frequently with samples arriving in advance of the main cargo, the further to facilitate forward trading.

The committee of the Baltic had, from the middle of the nineteenth century, held a lease on premises in South Sea House, and as this came to an end at around the turn of the century the committee cooperated with the management of the London Shipping Exchange for the purchase of a site where both bodies could be housed. This building was completed in 1903 in St Mary Axe. It is rather magnificent, with its vast trading floor and widely-spaced marble pillars. That it may convey (without intending any disrespect) a slightly religious impression to the stranger is probably in part due to the 'waiter' on his rostrum calling the names of members in a voice almost of incantation. The Baltic incidentally boasts a larger membership by far than any of the other markets.

Today the main centres of activity on the Baltic are the ship chartering and air freight markets, alongside which there also runs a thriving, though more limited, business in the actual sale of ships, done by certain of the brokers. The charter market is concerned with what are known as tramp ships – vessels which are chartered by the voyage, as distinct from the 'liners' which run to a schedule, picking up and discharging cargo at regular ports of call. Owners and charterers are represented on the market either direct or through the services of brokers or agents.

The air freight business was of course more recent in origin. It is said that the first air charterparty (chartering agreement) was issued in 1928 for a return flight from London to Cologne. After the Second World War the air freight business was organised through an Air Freight Advisory Committee, and in 1949 the Air Brokers Association was formed. Air charter is now very much a growth business, with passengers being carried in chartered aircraft to an increasing extent, so that the original business of the rapid transit of perishable or urgently required goods and equipment has added to it that of the movement of ship's crews, holidaymakers and even pilgrims.

Should you be fortunate enough to come across a copy of the *Public Ledger*, which is, incidentally, London's oldest newspaper, you will find listed the prices and market prospects for a whole Aladdin's cave of exotic products – oils, gums, spices and drugs (such as Tragacanth and Dragon's Blood) – all of which have their market somewhere within the small area of Mincing Lane. This is not simply a romantic return to earlier times before the intervention of synthetics, but a very direct reminder of the place still held by natural raw materials and their immediate derivatives in the commerce and (where drugs and even spices are concerned) the pharmacopaeia of today.

CHAPTER SIX

Insurance – The Companies

The notion of insurance is far from new. Prudence leads men to anticipate possible misfortune or misadventure and as far as maybe to protect themselves from its more dire effects. The vast and complicated business we see today developed from the concept of the spreading of risk among a number of insurers. 'Safety in numbers' is in a sense the backbone of insurance and of the actuarial information upon which risks are assessed and premiums calculated.

Earliest records speak first of insurance against marine risks, which in one form or another was taken out by merchant venturers before they set out for the unknown. Marine insurance on a more or less formalised basis was introduced into England by the Italians – the Lombards to whom we have already been introduced in an earlier chapter. We read of it as applied here in the preamble to an Act of Parliament of 1601 (see page 97). Accounts of this type of insurance are to be found in the records of the Italian bankers of the fourteenth century, when 'bottomry bonds' or loans against the security of a ship were turned around from being repayable on safe arrival to guaranteeing a sum in the event of non-arrival. From this device to true marine insurance was but a step and we find records of such cover being regulated and codified by various ordinances made in the sixteenth century in such centres as Florence and Antwerp (then a town of the Spanish Netherlands).

The rolls of the old Court of Admiralty show that marine insurance was in existence in England in the sixteenth century, though interestingly enough the earliest policies were made out in Italian, the various London underwriters adding their lines in English. We also see such a policy written in French, and underwritten in London, covering an Antwerp merchant in respect of a voyage to Central America.

Problems abounded, however. Disputes were frequent and for the most part were settled by arbitration, a process which grew out of the early law merchant and the 'courts of pie powder' (an anglicisation of *'pieds poudrés'* referring to the travelling merchants' dusty footwear). The Act of 1601 was passed in order to stabilise the situation, including as it did provision for the setting up of a special court to consider such cases. This position remained substantially unchanged until a reorganisation in the eighteenth century returned marine insurance cases to the care of the ordinary courts. We shall read in the next chapter of the development of this branch of insurance through the establishment of Lloyd's. Suffice it to say at this point that marine underwriting was shared between individuals who were frequently occupied in other directions and who wrote insurance as a profitable outlet for their own surplus funds. Though today they are full-time professionals who have banded together in syndicates, the Lloyd's underwriters still operate on this principle.

We find that life assurance has nearly as long a recorded history as marine insurance. The oldest record we have of a life policy in England was of that granted in 1588 on the life of a Mr William Gibbons in the sum of £382 6s 8d for twelve months. Unfortunately for the underwriters Gibbons died in the following year and before the twelve month term had elapsed.

Such short-term life policies became something of a commonplace, assuming importance in the eyes of, for example, backers of a merchant venturer undertaking a voyage, or of the lenders to a tradesman whose own skill was essential to the work, the proceeds of which were to repay the loan. Initially such policies could only be short term as the under-writers, too, were mortal. Something different had to be done if anything approaching whole-life assurance was to become a practicable proposition. One of the first ventures in this direction was the granting of a charter to the Amicable Society for a Perpetual Insurance Office by Queen Anne in 1706. Being a corporate body the Society was in a position to grant longer-term assurances. It operated by dividing the accumulated contributions of its members amongst the estates of members deceased since the last such division. The Society survived as an independent entity until 1866 when it was absorbed into the Norwich Union Assurance Society.

Curiously, of the three main branches of insurance in the days before the motor car and the aeroplane, fire was the last to appear on the scene in England in any organised form. It existed on the Continent in various municipalities (Hamburg was an example) where compensation was paid to property owners who suffered loss by fire, payment being made out of accumulated contributions paid as rates by the property owners within the city.

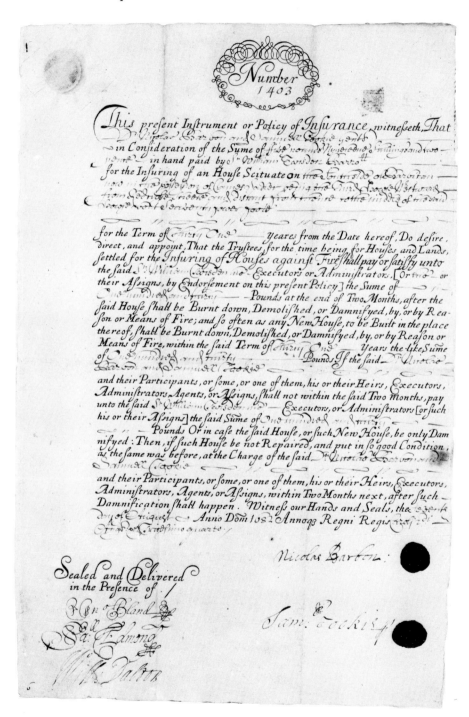

Number 1403

This present Instrument or Policy of Insurance, witnesseth, That *Nicholas Barbon and Samuel Cookie gents* in Consideration of the Sume of *five pounds nineteene shillings and two pence* in hand paid by *William Censden Carter* for the Insuring of an House Scituate on *the...*

for the Term of *Thirty One* yeares from the Date hereof, Do desire, direct, and appoint, That the Trustees, for the time being, for Houses and Lands, settled for the Insuring of Houses against Fire shall pay or satisfy unto the said *Sr William Censdenino* Executors or Administrators, [Or two or their Assigns, by Endorsement on this present Policy] the Sume of *One hundred and fifty* Pounds at the end of Two Months, after the said House shall be Burnt down, Demolished, or Damnifyed, by, or by Reason or Means of Fire; and so often as any New House, to be Built in the place thereof, shall be Burnt down, Demolished, or Damnifyed, by, or by Reason or Means of Fire, within the said Term of *Thirty One* Years the like Sume of *One hundred and fifty* Pounds If the said *Nicolao Barbon and Samuell Cookie*

and their Participants, or some, or one of them, his or their Heirs, Executors, Administrators Agents, or Assigns, shall not within the said Two Months, pay unto the said *Sr William Censdenino* Executors, or Administrators [or such his or their Assigns] the said Sume of *One hundred and fifty* Pounds Or in case the said House, or such New House, be only Damnifyed: Then, if such House be not Repaired, and put in so good Condition, as the same was before, at the Charge of the said *Sr Nicolao Barbon and Samuell Cookie*

and their Participants, or some, or one of them, his or their Heirs, Executors, Administrators, Agents, or Assigns, within Two Months next, after such Damnification shall happen. Witness our Hands and Seals, the *seventh day of August* Anno Dōm 1682 Annoqᵉ Regni Regis *Caroli Secundi Tricesimo quarto*

Nicolas Barbon

Sealed and Delivered in the Presence of

Geno Bland
Fa: Fleming
Will Falton

Same: Cookie

At the time of London's Great Fire of 1666, and despite previous only slightly less cataclysmic fires, there was no properly organised or managed fire insurance available. (By 'properly organised' we intend anything remotely resembling the facilities which may be obtained today.) All that did exist were a number of schemes run on a more or less charitable basis and dependent for their funds upon donations made in response to public appeals.

The first serious attempt at fire insurance on a more commercial and less quixotic basis was the Fire Office, situated at 'the back side of the Royal Exchange' where Nicholas Barbon and a few associates set themselves up in 1681 to insure brick-built houses at a rate of 6d per annum in the £ rent and timber houses for double this premium. Barbon no doubt had some technical knowledge of the relative vulnerability to fire of the various construction methods, since he was himself a speculative builder. (He was also the son of the renowned 'Praise-God Barbon' of Oliver Cromwell's day.) The venture must have been successful because we read that before long a guarantee fund had been raised. Known colloquially as the 'Phenix' from its emblem, the Fire Office survived for some years longer but seems to have disappeared by the end of the seventeenth century. (It had no connection, incidentally, with the Phoenix Assurance Company which was founded in 1782.)

Not that the risk of fire had been disregarded. In 1638 an application to form an insurance company or society had been approved, but it does not seem to have been followed up. The Corporation of the City of London itself had been made aware, by a letter from His Majesty to the Lord Mayor, of Charles II's own concern in the matter. The King in fact urged the City to issue and enforce requirements for building in materials less inflammable than exposed timber. Finally, in 1666, the year of the Great Fire, we are told that a group of army officers were executed, having been found guilty of plotting to fire the City.

In view of the extent of the Great Fire and the catastrophic damage it wrought, it would have been likely that had any such, relatively under-capitalised, societies been set up they would have been unable to meet the enormous number of claims which would have resulted. To this extent it may after all have been for the best that when, led by Barbon, insurance companies did emerge, it was into a period of being able to gather strength and experience without facing a major disaster.

Two years after Barbon's venture commenced operations the Friendly Society was set up, as a mutual fund. In this instance members paid a

Nicholas Barbon's signature on a fire insurance policy

White delin.   Taylor

Part of LONDON, as it appeared during the DREADFUL FIRE
in the Reign of CHARLES the IId. 1666.

deposit of 6*s* 8*d* per £100, followed by annual premiums of 1*s* 4*d*. Whilst the deposit was to be returned at the end of the period of the insurance, the contributor undertook meanwhile to subscribe up to 30*s* per £100 towards recompensing any other member suffering loss of property through fire.

In 1696 the two houses were joined by a third – the Amicable Contributors for Insuring Houses from Loss by Fire. This too was a mutual operation, on the same principle as the Friendly Society, and it continued successfully in business for some two hundred years; being absorbed into the Commercial Union Assurance Company in 1905. From its emblem the Amicable rapidly became known as the 'Hand in Hand' – a more digestible title and one perpetuated today happily enough in the title of the Commercial Union's international corporate journal.

The next development of significance was the establishment in 1710 of the Sun Fire Office, which is still with us today as the 'Sun' part of the Sun Alliance & London group. The Sun took over the earlier Exchange House Fire Office, brainchild of Charles Povey, which was an insurer of goods from loss by fire. The Sun insured premises as well as their contents and actually ran its own fire brigade. Two more newcomers in the field were the Union Fire Insurance Office, founded in 1714 with the blessing of the Hand in Hand, and the Westminster Fire Office, which was formed in 1717 by ex-members of the Hand in Hand who resented that company's move into the City.

The fire offices frequently employed their own men to act as firemen, although their work was mainly one of salvage until the arrival of portable fire-pumps and mains water. In London the Thames watermen frequently doubled-up in this capacity. The attractive marks of the offices, on plaques bearing their emblems, were affixed to the walls of the houses for which each was responsible and many of these may still be seen today on older buildings.

To return for a moment to Charles Povey. He may also be regarded as the father of the insurance agency which enables a company to insure risks in areas separate from its main sphere of operations by virtue of introductions provided by the agents. From these beginnings stemmed the whole apparatus of inspectors, surveyors and valuers acting for the insurance office by putting their special skills at its disposal in support of the agent, who frequently lacked the technical knowledge necessary for assessing a risk.

Perhaps at this point we should make an attempt at analysing the distinction – if such there is – between the words 'insurance' and 'assurance'.

The fire of London: an engraving in Thornton's *History of London*

The latter is the provision of a sum worked out on actuarial principles payable on the occurrence of an event such as the death of the assured, which is certain to happen sooner or later. Insurance, on the other hand, means the provision of compensation should a certain untoward occurrence take place (an accident or a fire) which, though not inevitable, remains a hazard. Today the two words tend to be interchangeable, and 'insurance' is often used to cover both applications.

The South Sea Bubble Act 1720 had as one of its objects the restriction of the formation of joint-stock companies without the prior granting of a charter. (We shall consider the Bubble episode in detail in Chapter 8.) In our present context, one of the Act's effects was to sanction the creation of two new insurance companies. These were the Royal Exchange Assurance and the London Assurance. We shall meet them again in the next chapter on Lloyd's; meanwhile their importance is that they were enabled not only to insure marine risks but to write life assurance on a corporate basis as distinct from that used by the mutuals. They were perhaps a little unenterprising here in that they seem only to have written short-term life cover. Nonetheless their creation as chartered companies was a milestone in the history of insurance in the City.

For the emergence of life assurance in anything like its modern form we have to wait until 1762 and the incorporation of the Society for Equitable Assurance on Lives and Survivorships, now the Equitable Life Assurance Society. Here, there was no share capital as such. The principle of the Society lay in a deed of settlement which envisaged a group, or society, of people who would be mutual contributors to life assurances. These would be based upon premiums worked out in accordance with calculations forecasting the life expectancy of various age-groups, and therefore the estimated endurance of the cover. Two side provisions were that in the event of death in an epidemic only a proportion of the sum assured would be immediately forthcoming (the balance to follow, with interest, 'as and when') and that any surplus of premium income would be divided amongst the policyholders.

It is interesting to note here that the 'mortality tables' on which the Equitable's premiums were based owed much to the calculations of Edmund Halley, the astronomer, who read a paper on the subject to the Royal Society in 1693. One drawback of Halley's mortality-rate forecasts was that, with no census of population as we know it today, they were based on a stable population figure.

However, despite the apparent odds stacked against it, the Equitable prospered. This was largely due to conservative management and a fortunate investment policy: its first distribution from surplus was not made until 1777. In the closing years of the eighteenth century and the early years of the nineteenth there were numerous formations of life assurance societies; of these the Phoenix with its sister company the Pelican, the London Life, the Eagle and the Provident are worthy of mention here, along with Scotland's first – the Scottish Widows Fund, founded in 1815.

With maritime insurance going its separate way via Lloyd's and the two 1720 creations, the next step was a coming together of the fire and life companies into what were to become known as composite offices. In the first two decades of the nineteenth century many new companies were incorporated, which from the outset transacted both fire and life business. The monopoly situation in the marine field came to an end in 1824 with the

London fire engines in the nineteenth century

granting of a charter to the Alliance Assurance Company. This was the creation of the redoubtable Nathan Rothschild. The 1824 Act removed the restriction on the writing of marine insurance by corporate bodies, which had been instituted by the Bubble Act of 1720, and which had permitted only the Royal Exchange and the London, as companies, to enter the marine field. (Lloyd's underwriters, being individuals, were not so restricted, as we shall see in the next chapter.)

From 1824 onwards it was possible for the true composite, transacting all forms of insurance, to come into being. Amongst the more notable of these companies was the Commercial Union, which commenced marine insurance activity in 1863. This company (today one of the largest of the composites) was founded very shortly after the Tooley Street warehouse fire which destroyed a number of riverside properties in Southwark, together with a vast store of produce contained there. This disaster cost the insurers over £1 million, and its repercussions included the formation of several new companies as well as the institution of the London Fire Brigade. In 1844 the Joint Stock Companies Act (the forerunner of a series of Companies Acts), which amongst other things went a long way towards regulating the establishment and the capitalisation of insurance companies, was passed. The Act required the registration of new companies and the annual compilation of a return to be sent to the Registrar of Friendly Societies. Unfortunately the Act did not go far enough, and there was for a time a distinction between companies incorporated before its passing, and those (more strictly regulated) which came into being afterwards. It is important, however, not only as an attempt at 'modern' company legislation but as being, at least in part, instrumental in bringing about the conditions needed for the establishment of the forerunners of today's very large composite insurance companies.

The final category of insurance we have to consider is accident insurance which not unnaturally grew with the increasing complexity, and potential for causing bodily harm, of machinery and means of locomotion introduced during the Industrial Revolution. The railways and the steam-driven plant coming into use in factories and textile mills brought with them their own problems of personal injury. The earliest insurances written were, for the most part, in the nature of personal accident policies, issued in favour of individuals. The liability of employers towards the safety of their workforce was but gradually accepted and we have to wait until the Employers' Liability Act 1881 for the first firm legislation on the matter. This was followed in 1906 by the Workmen's Compensation Act which obliged employers to pay weekly a sum in compensation to any employee

Nathan Meyer de Rothschild: watercolour by Robert Dighton

suffering incapacity as a result of an accident occurring at work, the employee's negligence notwithstanding. One of the consequences of the Act was the formation of a number of new accident insurance companies, which were often inexperienced in the field.

Meanwhile the established fire offices were opening up branches to deal with accident insurance in addition to their traditional business. As a result, by the outbreak of the First World War there had already been many amalgamations and the large composite insurance company dealing in all forms of risk was well established. The process has been continuing though not perhaps with the same degree of assimilation that we have seen in the banking sphere where the retail market is now dominated by the 'Big Four'. However, in non-life insurance the market tends now to be led by ten or so very large groups.

In the accident field, motor insurance has probably been the branch most fraught with risk of loss to the insurer. The Road Traffic Act 1930 made third party insurance mandatory for all motorists, and the rapid growth of private and business motoring brought new companies into being, often competing with the older-established houses by way of cutting premium rates to their customers. Inevitably this form of competition caused failures, of which the most serious and far-reaching in its consequences was that of the Vehicle and General in 1971.

Not all insurance is concerned with compensation for the effects of some foreseeable yet not inevitable misfortune. The life assurance policy for example has of recent years been taken as the basis for a whole gamut of what could properly be described as investment programmes, both corporate and personal. The provision of a pension, of an income on retirement and even of a stake in a property portfolio are all feasible through various schemes which are effected via the purchase of units in a 'basket' of investments in various fields. All of this is backed by a life policy whose premiums provide the finance for the investment. This is of particular significance for the self-employed, who for obvious reasons are not participants in any ments in various fields. All of this is backed by a life policy whose premiums for providing funds for possible medical treatment, in addition to providing for their dependants by means of unit-linked life policies, is a matter of great importance.

The continuing development of what is still very much a growth business, as technology and sometimes pure human waywardness seem to produce an unending variety of new hazards, has drawn the industry together into a number of corporate bodies, certain of which ought to be mentioned here. In 1917 the British Insurance Association was founded to bring together

Lead fire mark of the Hand in Hand fire office

the numerous companies up and down the country and ensure that in matters of common concern they were able to speak with one voice. However, this move was anticipated by the life offices, amongst whom a Scottish association had been formed as early as 1841 and its English counterpart, the Life Offices Association, in London in 1889. There is a separate organisation representing the industrial life offices, which is concerned to a great extent in that area in which its members are brought into contact with government and with legislation on a national and, particularly, a social level.

Finally, mention must be made of the Chartered Insurance Institute. This body is concerned primarily with educational matters affecting the actual people occupied in the business of insurance. Granted its charter in 1912, it has its headquarters (including a library, lecture theatre and a delightful museum of old 'fire marks' and equipment) in Aldermanbury Square near the Guildhall.

In terms of their financial development the composite insurance companies have progressed to the point where the relatively few (and by any standards very large) main protagonists have obtained such a stature as to make their presence felt in other related fields. This is especially noticeable when we consider their need to invest the great sums of money coming regularly into their coffers by way of life-assurance premiums and the like. These sums have to earn their keep and yet leave sufficient liquidity to meet claims which arise with disconcerting suddenness. (The sea and the air do not hold the monopoly of disaster potential as the explosion in a chemical plant at Flixborough in 1974 shows.) How the investment policy of the great companies affects other parts of the interlocking City, and what the near future may hold in store for the whole will be a major theme in the concluding chapter.

CHAPTER SEVEN

Insurance – Lloyd's

'Individually we are underwriters, collectively we are Lloyd's.' The Corporation of Lloyd's was brought into being under an Act of Parliament in 1871. It is not a company in the accepted sense of the term, and the underwriting members of Lloyd's take unlimited liability in respect of insurance risks accepted by them. Originally these underwriters acted purely in an individual capacity, often accepting insurance risks as a sideline to their main activities. Today they are grouped into syndicates and operate collectively, the better able to deal in the huge sums of money now involved. Insurance placed at Lloyd's may cover almost any sort of risk, though it does not include financial guarantees of any kind, and only fairly recently was long-term life assurance brought in. The four major markets at Lloyd's now are marine, non-marine, motor and aviation.

To seek the origin of this unique institution, the total premium income of whose members now exceeds £6 million each working day, we again return to the coffee houses and in particular to that run by Mr Edward Lloyd (or Loyd), whose house in Tower Street is first referred to in 1688. This was the year of the 'Glorious Revolution' which brought the Dutch King William and his Queen Mary jointly to England's throne. With the exception of the short reign (1702–14) of Queen Anne it marked the end of the Stuart era, which had itself been interrupted by the Civil War and the Commonwealth under Oliver Cromwell and his son Richard. Though not then by any means new, insurance was very much to the fore, notably in respect of marine hazards in those troubled times.

Arranging cover then was a matter of individuals acting as brokers taking policies round the wealthy merchants and others in the expectation that some would add their names to them in return for a share of the premiums. There was as yet no central location to which all those seeking or arranging cover might come, and in common with the other emerging markets the venue was the coffee house and Mr Lloyd's in particular. There is no evidence that Lloyd himself underwrote any insurance, (he described himself as a 'coffee man') but he undoubtedly took much interest, even to the extent of publishing a regular bulletin thrice weekly. Before his death in 1713 he also published a shipping list, the forerunner of *Lloyd's List*, which was first issued in 1734 as a weekly and later a bi-weekly publication.

During the early years of the eighteenth century there was an enormous amount of private wealth in London, and those who possessed it were not always particularly conservative as to how they employed it. The distinction between enterprise and speculation (gambling) has always been a pretty fine one and not easy to draw. In what were approaching boom conditions the confidence man and the hawker of prospectuses flourished. The most notorious example of such activity was the scandal of the South Sea Company which culminated in a major collapse in 1720 – the bursting of the 'South Sea Bubble' (see Chapter 8). In that same year an Act was passed, known irreverently as the 'Bubble Act', amongst whose provisions was the granting of charters to two newly-formed bodies – the London Assurance and the Royal Exchange Assurance companies. At the same time all other companies or partnerships were prohibited from underwriting any marine insurance. However, the underwriters gathered at Lloyd's (now moved to Lombard Street) took responsibility, without limit as to personal liability, only for themselves and not for each other; thus they were acting in the legal sense as individuals and their activities did not fall within the scope of the Act, which expressly excluded 'private and particular persons'.

The South Sea Bubble and other less famous but no less catastrophic episodes did little or nothing to lessen the urge to gamble. Under the same roof at Mr Lloyd's there mixed the serious men seeking a premium income as a way of making a return on their capital and the out-and-out gamblers who would place what amounted to a bet on the non-occurrence of almost any eventuality. This was a situation which inevitably became less and less acceptable to the former. In 1769 therefore they moved into the 'New Lloyd's Coffee House' in Pope's Head Alley and commenced publication of their own *New Lloyd's List*. Here, they confined their activities to marine insurance only, eschewing all other types of risk. Thus, of the four main Lloyd's markets marine is the oldest.

Such was the growth in importance of this business that after a scant two years the 'New' coffee house proved too small to accommodate all who gathered there to transact business. In 1771 the underwriters formed a Committee of nine which was charged with responsibility for finding new permanent headquarters. Of those concerned, seventy-nine brokers, under-

Lloyd's coffee house in the Royal Exchange, 1798

writers and interested merchants each contributed £100 to fund the acquisition and the moneys were paid into an account at the Bank of England. After a further three years rooms were secured in the Royal Exchange, which were furnished and fitted out in keeping. Thus the first step was taken towards the establishment of the modern Lloyd's. Credit for much of this was due to the energy and leadership of John Julius Angerstein, who has, quite justly, been dubbed the 'Father of Lloyd's'.

Under its elected committee the society of underwriters gradually took on a more cohesive form. New entrants were subject to approval and only members and their immediate associates were permitted entry into the underwriters' room. The society continued to do an increasing turnover throughout the alarums and excursions of the American War of Independence and the prolonged war against France. In 1871 this steady progress was rewarded by the granting of formal incorporation by Act of Parliament and this original Act has from time to time been amended in the light of changing conditions. Now the Corporation of Lloyd's acts as the proprietor of the market's premises and it lays down the very strict regulations governing entrance to, and the conduct of, business done on the market, without

89

itself undertaking any of that business. The Committee continues responsible for everyday management and administration.

During this formative period, certain events of significance ought not to pass unnoticed. In 1779 the first standard form of marine policy was drafted and agreed. It differs, actually, very little from that in use today even to the inclusion of such references as that to 'pirates, rovers, etc.', words not without relevance in our uncomfortable era of hijacking.

A further organisational step was taken with the first appointment in 1796 of three Masters, who were *inter alia* responsible for the, by then greatly increasing and widening, intelligence network. These appointments were followed in 1804 by that of Mr John Bennett, Jnr, as the first full-time Secretary of Lloyd's. Seven years later there came the signing by all members of a trust deed giving Lloyd's a formal constitution. (This was coincidentally accompanied by an increase in the subscription.)

Today the Committee of Lloyd's numbers sixteen, of whom four retire by rotation each year, being eligible to stand for re-election after a lapse of not less than twelve months. Its main responsibilities are the election of new members, and ensuring the financial standing of all existing members (of whom there are more than 1400). In this they are aided by the annual audit of all members, which was first introduced in 1908 as a voluntary gesture by the members themselves. Meanwhile, Mr Bennett's current successor is the Secretary-General, who is in charge of a headquarters staff of some 2000.

In 1793 a French frigate *La Lutine* surrendered to the British at Toulon. She was then commissioned into the Royal Navy as HMS *Lutine*, and in 1799 was running a cargo of bullion from Yarmouth Roads to Hamburg when she foundered on the sands off Vlieland in Holland. Her precious cargo (valued variously between £250,000 and over £1 million) was insured at Lloyd's and the claim was met in full. Several salvage attempts have since been made on this difficult piece of coastline, and to date some £100,000 in specie has been recovered along with some of the ship's thirty-nine cannon, her rudder (now fashioned into a table and chair in the library at Lloyd's), her captain's watch and her ship's bell. Moneys received from disposal of the salvaged bullion were invested over the years 1871–90 in a chain of signal stations and other forms of communication direct with Lloyd's.

The Lutine Bell, which was raised in 1859, is now mounted over the rostrum in the underwriting room. Contrary to popular belief it is not rung solely to announce the loss of a ship but it is struck before any an-

The Lutine Bell

nouncement of unusual importance – two strokes for good news and one for bad.

Lloyd's connection with the sea and with sailoring in all its aspects has been exemplified time and again. In 1794 came the news of Lord Howe's victory over the French in the 'Glorious First of June'. A general meeting was straightaway called at Lloyd's, with a view to raising a fund for the relief of sufferers in the action or their dependants. The fund raised altogether £21,282 and *The Times* reported that 'with the liberality which will ever distinguish that body of men [they] in less than one hour subscribed a thousand guineas'. The playwright Sheridan also contributed over £1300 from a special performance of one of his works, and Lord Howe himself gave the whole of his prize money resulting from the action. Subscribers also presented plate and other valuables to officers of Howe's fleet, including the Harvey Tureen, a splendid piece of silver given to John Harvey, captain of HMS *Brunswick*. In perspective, however, welcome as it was as a stimulus to national morale, Howe's victory was not enough to prevent the French grain convoy from America reaching port with its precious cargo.

No commentary on this period of Lloyd's history would be complete without reference to the society's links with Lord Nelson, visible evidence of which may be seen in the Nelson collection, which includes letters, insignia and the log of the frigate *Euryalus*. This contains a graphic description of the Battle of Trafalgar in which the Admiral lost his life and which was preceded by the hoist of the historic signal 'England expects that every man will do his duty' as recorded in *Euryalus*'s deck log. A further signal ordered a close engagement. Lloyd's connection with Nelson actually began in 1798 when no less than £38,436 was raised in order to bring comfort to the casualties of the Battle of Aboukir Bay (the Nile) and to their dependants. An additional vote was approved for £500 for the Admiral 'to be laid out in plate', and some of this silver may be seen in the collection.

The tradition of providing money and gifts to those involved in action at sea was given more formal guise in the establishment of the Patriotic Fund set up in 1803 (two years before Trafalgar). After 1809 the practice of making presentations in kind was discontinued and the Fund, which is still in existence, has from that time on concentrated on offering monetary support to those disabled in naval actions. The old custom of presentations was, however, given new life in a different form with the gift of Lloyd's medals in remembrance of individual acts of bravery at sea, not only in war but in the saving of life or property from the hazards of the sea.

In 1838 there could have been a major disaster when the Royal Exchange was totally destroyed by fire. In fact, and his name merits recording, a subscriber called Guthrie took charge of salvage operations and was instrumental in saving the major part of the records, including most of the Committee minute books. From then until 1844, when it returned to the rebuilt Royal Exchange, the society took temporary headquarters in South Sea House, situated at the corner of Threadneedle Street and Bishopsgate and home of the Baltic. The new accommodation in the Royal Exchange duly received for the first time the more official-sounding title of Lloyd's Subscription Rooms; the soubriquet 'Coffee House' had tended still to apply to the rooms in the earlier building.

Of the other main markets making up the bulk of the business transacted at Lloyd's, the non-marine was instituted in or about 1887 when Cuthbert Heath, whose name lives today in C. E. Heath & Company, first wrote policies for business other than marine risks. The innovation proved successful, and non-marine insurance accounted for much of the great increase in business underwritten in the closing years of the nineteenth century. Today it represents over half of total premium income. Though this type of risk was first considered highly speculative (conjuring up memories in the more conservative breasts of the bad old coffee house days), Heath proceeded successfully to underwrite policies for such subtleties as loss of profits resulting from fire, and to initiate block policies for jewellers and the like. He was a man of considerable vision, and is also credited with the introduction of the first policies of reinsurance. These were originally written for an English company's American business. Reinsurance is a method of sharing the risk on a large insurance, or one where a claim might be unusually heavy. The insurer accepts the risk himself and covers a proportion of it with others, though he alone remains in a contractual position *vis-à-vis* the policy holder.

Perhaps the most spectacular vindication of Heath's inventiveness was the way in which Lloyd's members were able to meet very large claims arising from the enormous damage sustained in the San Francisco earthquake and fire in 1906. (There is a true story told of a telephone caller to a San Francisco number who, when he complained about the bad connection, was politely told by the lady operator that she was doing her best, but that 'we are having an earthquake here'.) Not satisfied with his introduction of reinsurance, Heath then conceived the idea of excess insurance. This came into operation only when the giver of the original cover had to meet an exceptionally large claim and after he had paid that part of such a claim for which he was responsible. Excess is now very much a part of the whole insurance complex.

The first aviation insurance in standard form was accepted at Lloyd's

Lloyd's underwriting room in Lime Street

in 1911 – two years after Bleriot's first air crossing of the English Channel and one year after the tragic death in an air crash of the Hon C. S. Rolls, partner of Henry Royce. Nowadays Lloyd's underwriters are able to arrange cover for both flying and motoring risks by way of making the facilities of the two markets available to non-member brokers. Both markets are growing ones, given the apparently unstoppable increase in road transport and – despite an enviable safety record – the increasing costs of even the comparatively rare air disaster with larger and more complex aircraft involved.

We should perhaps turn the clock back a little here, to look at the growth and development of *Lloyd's Register of Shipping*. This was the creation of a group of underwriters and first came into being in the coffee house days in 1760. The *Register* reached its third edition in 1775 and it was to this issue that the origin of the term 'A1' conveying excellence can be attributed. In the classification used, the letter A meant a thoroughly sound hull, and the figure 1 referred to the quality and state of rigging and equipment; hence an 'A1' or first class ship.

The method of classification used by these underwriters in compiling their *Register* – the 'Green Book' – led eventually to disagreement with some of the ship-owners who duly commenced publication of their own register of shipping in 1779. This rather anomalous situation persisted until 1834 when the two bodies joined forces, with lack of finance as a common spur, and in that year *Lloyd's Register of Shipping* was incorporated as a body separate from the Corporation of Lloyd's itself. The two do in fact co-operate very closely and members of the Committee of Lloyd's serve on the *Register*'s Committee as well. More recently, the *Register* and the newly-established Lloyd's of London Press (also publishers, among other things, of authoritative law reports) agreed to share a computerised intelligence service related to shipping information. It remains a fact though that *Lloyd's Register* is an independent body, occupying its own premises in Fenchurch Street – the heart of the City's shipping area – with its own management and staff.

The Corporation of Lloyd's itself remained in the Royal Exchange until as recently as 1928 when it transferred to a new building in Leadenhall Street, which was opened by King George V and Queen Mary. Eight years later the adjacent Royal Mail House, built on the site of East India House, was also acquired. One further move was to come. In 1957 Lloyd's moved into its new premises in Lime Street, with the 'Bridge of Sighs' connecting it with Royal Mail House on the opposite side. The underwriting room was actually transferred to the new building on 8 April 1958, two days short of thirty years after the move from the Royal Exchange which brought to a close that splendid building's long association with the City's markets.

In this account we have so far confined ourselves to a general history of the development of this unique institution and it is probably time now to look a little closer at some of the detail of how its business is done, and how it came to be done this way. The underwriters themselves are now full-time professionals rather than wealthy merchants looking for an additional outlet for their funds. For some time past, the underwriters have tended to group themselves into syndicates, the better to handle ever-increasing figures and spread the burden. There are currently some three hundred of these syndicates, each managed by an underwriting agent and each varying very much in numbers of members.

The syndicate system arose in quite early days out of the method which an underwriter (who would probably have been occupied in other business as well) used for arranging for associates or acquaintances to join him in 'writing a line' on a policy and thereby assuming the liability for a share of the total risk. The method was formalised, and strengthened, when in 1840 the Committee laid down that all names appearing on a Lloyd's policy must be those of members of the society, whether underwriting themselves or through an agent. Increasing business made this system extremely burdensome, to the extent that in 1916 a centralised Signing Office was set up, which came under the purview of the Committee in 1924. Now the policies are signed in this office on behalf of the syndicates which have indicated their preparedness to underwrite them on the broker's slip which he will have taken round amongst them. Settlements of premiums and claims between the syndicates and the brokers are also made centrally, once each month.

The size of the syndicates, or the emergence of such really large ones as are seen today, was a direct consequence of the growth of the non-marine business in the closing years of the last century and the early years of this. In turn this expansion has led to an increase in the number of members, all of whom must meet certain very stringent requirements as to personal standing and financial strength. In 1968 the decision was taken to admit citizens of countries outside the Commonwealth, and the historic decision to admit lady members followed one year later.

We saw on an earlier page that long-term life assurance (that is, for periods of over seven years) was a new departure. This exclusion from the catalogue of cover available was quite logical and stemmed from the personal nature of underwriting at Lloyd's. Because of this, it was not possible to guarantee that all or any of those underwriting a life policy would themselves outlive the assured nor was there any ready way to allow for new members joining a syndicate during the term of the policy. The situation regarding life assurance was altered with the creation in 1971 of Lloyd's Life Assurance Ltd – a company with a capital of £4 million and with members subscribing by way of their Premium Trust Fund, which was itself set up in 1908.

The underwriters themselves do not have any contact with those seeking cover. All business coming their way is channelled through one of the recognised brokers. He will make contact with more than one syndicate in order to obtain the best terms for his client and after one syndicate has given a lead by quoting a rate, the broker will contact as many others as may be needed to share the full amount of cover required. From this we may see that members of the society are in healthy competition amongst themselves to offer the keenest terms (and any subsequent claim falls on them as individuals with unlimited liability), but in cooperation as to the spread of the financial load over many shoulders. Though it anticipated the founding of the Corporation by many years, the preamble to an Act of Parliament passed during the reign of Elizabeth I sets out the principle very aptly: 'it cometh to pass that on the loss or perishing of any ship there followeth not the undoing of any man, but the loss lighteth rather more easily upon many than heavilie upon fewe. . . .'

CHAPTER EIGHT

The Stock Exchange

Some three-quarters of the adult population of Britain are investors of money via the Stock Exchange. Many are quite unaware of the fact, since the investments are made on their behalf by way of life assurance and membership of pension funds. And the marketing and transfer from hand to hand of shares in quoted companies and in units of government stock constitutes another and very important part of the City's complicated trading web.

We can trace the beginnings of the story back as far as the northern voyage of Chancellor and Willoughby and the Muscovy Company which was its outcome. The merchant venturers needed finance for their explorations. As in the case of insurance underwriting, finance and the risk of all or part of the money being lost had to be spread amongst a number of individuals. In the truest sense the Muscovy Company was the first recorded joint-stock company, wherein the shareholders made their contributions in cash or in kind to the 'stock'. The East India Company constituted a further landmark in that after the first few voyages, for which funds were raised each time on a somewhat *ad hoc* basis, the company found itself with a residue of permanent capital. This quite quickly produced very pleasant yields for the fortunate stockholders, as well as increasing the market value of the stock, thus facilitating the raising of loans by the company at favourable rates of interest.

The oldest company still listed on the Stock Exchange is the New River Company. It owes its origin to a scheme of the then Earl of Bedford for draining the Fens, and in so doing providing London with its first proper supply of fresh water. The company was incorporated in 1609 and survived as a provider and purifier of water until early in this century when it became a part of what was then the Metropolitan Water Board. As an owner of property – most of which is in the area around Sadler's Wells Theatre – it survives to this day. The second-oldest listed company is none other than the Hudson's Bay Company, which we have already encountered in Chapter 2.

The raising of money by subscription was a feature of the later years of the seventeenth century, and many and various were the enterprises to which the wealthy were invited to contribute. They ranged from the original issue of capital in the Bank of England in 1694, when no less than £1,200,000 was raised in two weeks, to such diverse businesses as fire insurance, mining and smelting, and others which appear to have been of a rather mysterious nature and which not surprisingly had short lives.

Arms of the Hudson's Bay Company

At this time, and indeed for some years to come, wealth tended to be concentrated in relatively few hands. This, combined with the lack, very often, of avenues in which surplus funds might 'earn their keep', encouraged the more speculative kind of investment in which there was, more often than not, a strong element of pure gambling. So these new ventures, or 'adventures' as they were at the time described in prospectuses, covered a whole catalogue of the weird and wonderful.

In passing, it is worthy of record that the first national lottery was also subscribed for in 1694, the year of the birth of the Bank of England and the National Debt. The latter was the procedure whereby the Crown raised funds by inviting subscriptions from the public. Because of the status of the guarantor of redemption of these loans on their maturity the issues came to be known as 'gilt-edged'. In practice the funding process tends to be by way of further issues of government stock.

There was as yet no central market place for dealing in shares in the new-fangled joint-stock companies. Brokers were of course already a well-established species but they continued to operate, bringing sellers and purchasers together in the hope of making a commission, in a variety of fields. The specialised broker in stocks and shares had not yet come on to the scene. In fact the activities of the brokers caused a certain amount of unrest and hostility, to the extent that in 1673 an Act was passed which sought to regulate the conduct of their affairs.

Here the jobber comes into the picture, and since he is still something of a mystery to those not well versed in Stock Exchange practice we should perhaps consider him in some detail at this point. In essence, a jobber is a wholesaler (in this instance of stocks and shares) who trades as a principal on his own account. He holds tranches of shares in more than one company and is prepared to sell from his own holding or to buy into it as appears favourable. In this way the jobber acts as a most useful and efficient buffer between the market and the investors. Today jobbers are relatively few in number, having merged over recent years into larger units, the better to deal with the much greater sums involved in the performance of their function in a market where over 9000 different issues are traded. It can easily be seen that even when specialising as they do in a limited number of issues the jobbers run enormous risks in terms of price movements amongst the shares they hold. To be in a position to deal adequately with such a situation, therefore, a much larger capital base is needed today than used to be the case.

It is the jobber who makes a market in a share. When approached by a broker – who does not at this point identify himself as buyer or seller – the jobber quotes two prices, buyer's and seller's, and also on occasion may indicate the number of shares for which such prices hold good in one deal. In this way a market is assured at all times and the brokers need call on only a very few jobbers, each of whom names his own prices, to ascertain the marketability of the share in which his client wishes to deal, and to quote him a fair price with minimum delay. The jobber as a breed is unique to London, by the way, and on other large exchanges such as New York the more important brokerage houses combine the two functions.

The jobbers got away to a rather inauspicious start. They were accused –

sometimes no doubt with a measure of justification – of rigging the market in making their quotations. Some even were suspected of making prices for shares they did not actually hold, with the intent to acquire them elsewhere at a lower price were their offer for sale to be accepted. Another practice, though this was by no means confined to the jobbers, was that of 'buying more than all'. Here a syndicate would buy all or as much of a particular stock as their combined wealth would allow, at the same time offering a fee 'for refuse' to any who undertook to sell them further shares in the same stock. Some at least of the takers of this fee would have been speculators who hoped to acquire the shares themselves in order to deliver them to the syndicate. To meet this obligation they could, due to the squeeze, find themselves compelled to buy at a considerable premium. And the sellers to these unhappy men? The original syndicate, no doubt.

In 1696 Parliament was moved to set up a committee to look into the whole practice of jobbing and broking. In consequence in the following year an Act was passed 'to restrain the number and ill-practice of brokers and stock jobbers'. This applied to brokers across the board and included those in commodities. They were to be approved and licensed by the Lord Mayor and the Court of Aldermen; their numbers were to be limited to one hundred and all must take an oath to 'truly and faithfully execute and perform the office and employment of a broker between party and party. . . .' The licensed brokers were provided with silver medals bearing on one side the royal cypher and on the other the arms of the City. The medals were struck at the Royal Mint and several survive, some of which are displayed in the council anteroom of the present Stock Exchange. (A nice gesture was the issue to all members in 1972 of a medal based on the original design to commemorate the opening of the new Stock Exchange building.)

The licensed brokers were called on for an admission fee of £2 and a deposit of £500. They were enjoined to keep proper books, to restrict their commissions to a maximum of 10*s* per cent and never to deal on their own account. The Act of 1697 was to continue in force for three years, and after being renewed for a further seven was allowed to lapse. This was possibly on account of the storm of protest it occasioned amongst those excluded from the fortunate few licensed brokers – a protest which rumbled on for years with petition and counter-petition. In fairness to those not granted licences, one hundred does seem a very meagre number, given the extent of commercial activity in the City at the time.

The brokers and certainly the dealers, or jobbers, appear to have been meeting regularly in the Royal Exchange together with dealers in commodities, bill brokers and others with business to do. We know, too, that they met in the coffee houses and that Garraway's and Jonathan's were those most favoured. By the beginning of the eighteenth century they were established in their own walk in the Royal Exchange, where they seem to have made themselves unpopular on account of the general uproar which accompanied their dealings. It was said that they 'caused the walls to resound with the din of new projects'. There was a general exodus of the stockbrokers and jobbers from the Royal Exchange and numbers of them took to meeting in Change Alley just outside. (Change Alley still exists as a covered passage between Lombard Street and Cornhill.) However, they caused sufficient obstruction there as to have been the subject

Garraway's coffee house: an engraving in *Walford's London*

of hostile proclamations by the City Corporation. The term 'kerb dealings', meaning out-of-hours trading, which is now common to all the markets thus has its own literal origin.

Of the several coffee houses frequented for meetings and discussion and used as locations for the posting of notices of proposed new subscriptions to various 'adventures', Garraway's deserves a particular mention, as the birthplace of the Stock Exchange *Official List*. In 1697 a broker, one John Castaing, commenced the practice of displaying at Garraway's a list of current quotations, compiled in fact by his son. For the time it must have been pretty comprehensive; it included prices of commodities as well as those of shares, and was published twice weekly. After Castaing's death his sister continued publication of the list, in partnership first with Richard Shergold and later with Peter Smithson, who themselves were both brokers. Castaing's modest little publication was the direct forerunner of today's *Official List*, which runs now into many newsprint pages.

In the latter half of the eighteenth century we find the brokers occupied chiefly with dealings in home and overseas government issues. That there was not more business done in what today would be called the private sector was probably attributable to two causes. In the first place there was at the time little need for subscription to private ventures. With the exception of major utilities such as canals private industry was still very much at the level of the self-financing family concern, having little need for funds from outside, other than occasional bank finance or the discounting of its trade bills. The second reason for this seeming lack of interest in commercial joint-stock ventures was the aftermath of the rise and collapse of the South Sea Bubble.

We have already made mention of the Bubble in the context of insurance and the Act of 1720 (Chapters 6 and 7). Naturally the episode had a more direct bearing on the stock market and in particular on the notion of government involvement in commercial ventures. In 1698 the government of the day had itself floated a new company, the General Society, 'for the service of the Crown of England' with a promised dividend to subscribers of 8 per cent. After only four years, however, it was amalgamated with the older East India Company, to form the United East India Company. But the notion of public subscription in government or national enterprises lived on. With the heavy accumulation of the National Debt, which after the War of the Spanish Succession amounted to £9 million, the possibility of some form of public involvement was again mooted, this time by none other than the Chancellor of the Exchequer, Robert Hardy.

Accordingly in 1711 it was announced that a new joint-stock company would be formed, with the resounding title of 'The Governor and Company of Merchants of Great Britain trading to the South Seas and other parts of America, and for encouraging the Fishery'. The National Debt was to be refinanced out of the issue of shares in this company.

Had trading profits been forthcoming (which unfortunately, and with the recommencement of war with Spain after a very short period of peace, they were not), then who knows what benefits might have accrued? Certainly, at the time of its launch, there were many, including some in high positions, who honestly thought that the company would be a commercial success and would even transform the National Debt into a national profit. The capital of this extremely popular venture was increased twice in rapid succession, in 1715 and 1717 and, after the second increase it stood at no less than £12 million. This was no mean figure, and in retrospect not a healthy one either, considering that this sum amounted to over half of the total moneys invested in all joint-stock companies at the time, including the Bank of England and the East India Company.

But this was by no means the end of the company's growth, nor of its unfortunate influence. By the spring of 1720 its capital stood at the astounding figure of £43 million, with not a hope of showing a profit on such a vast borrowing from a gullible public and very little chance of ever servicing such an inflated capital. Perhaps, though, a lesson was in the course of being learnt from the collapse of the Banque Royale in Paris, which was a comparable near-fraudulent exercise in share-pushing controlled by the renegade Scot, John Law. In any event, the price of shares in the South Sea Company traced an erratic course during the year 1720 between a high point of £1000 in July, though a breathtaking plunge to £175 two months later, to a low of £125 at the year's end.

The position and the reigning 'investment fever' were made worse in many ways by the passing of the somewhat inept 'Bubble Act' in June 1720. This sought to prevent the flotation of any company without a Royal Charter, and imposed a maximum fine of £500 on any broker dealing in such a company's shares. (One by-product of the Act, as we have seen in Chapter 6, was the granting of charters to two companies for the transaction of marine insurance.) The Act appears to have been a rather naïve attempt at creating something approaching a complete monopoly for the vast and by now quite uncontrollable South Sea Company. Such was the height by then of investment fever that ever wilder schemes were launched almost daily in Change Alley, in spite of the penalties laid down in the Act, which seems to have been almost totally disregarded.

The inevitable collapse came later in the same year as the Act was passed and was followed by a full investigation carried out by a committee appointed by Parliament. As the outcome of the committee's deliberations, it was agreed that the Bank of England and the East India Company should each take up £9 million of the South Sea Company's shares and that the company continue to trade under a new board of directors. This decision was in fact in line with the earlier recommendation of Walpole, the Prime Minister, who had himself been one of the more fortunate speculators. In its new guise the company continued to operate for a number of years, though, perhaps fortunately, it never attracted further public attention.

If we have devoted a fair amount of space to the misfortunes of the South Sea Company, it is probably justified by the example it holds forth of a combination of almost all the things that can go wrong. When a new venture is launched, becomes over-fashionable in the eyes of investors and is controlled by those too concerned with cash and with the delights which cash may bring, the collapse sooner or later is inevitable. That such débâcles are happily rare is a reflection of the control and the discipline which have evolved over the years since the first heady days of speculation in 'adventures'. True, there have been more recent scandals – amongst the more notorious those involving Horatio Bottomley, Clarence Hatry, Peter Baker and others – but the system which has been fashioned in the course of a couple of centuries to protect the investor (very often from himself) is another example of the City's powers of self-discipline.

And so with the memory of the South Sea Bubble still strong, the market turned its emphasis towards shares in government debt as distinct from commercial issues. Subscription to overseas loans was also promoted, to the extent that the Prime Minister, Walpole, brought in an Act which sought to monitor this market by requiring a Royal licence for all who dealt in it. As to the home 'funds', as these government issues were coming to be called, their size and frequency of issue necessitated the accompanying offer of such side-benefits as lottery tickets or annuities. Thus it came about that in 1781 a number of separate 3 per cent annuity issues were lumped together into one 3 per cent Consolidated Bank Annuities Fund, and so 'Consols' came into being as a government stock.

This emphasis on government issues brought on to the scene the Government Contractor. He was a person – or it might be a corporation – who tendered competitively for the facility to buy tranches of a new stock for his own book, being in a position to guarantee beforehand that he had investors ready to take it up. In this way, we see the beginnings of the practice of underwriting an issue. Today this forms a part of the manifold activities of the merchant banks, and it has a very strong bearing on new issues in the equities market as well as in gilt-edged. When too high a proportion of an issue is reported as having been 'left with the under-writers' this is a gloomy omen indeed.

In the context of financing the National Debt it is well worth mentioning at this point an ingenious idea which, if in the event it proved not totally effective, is nevertheless of some importance to our review of the Stock Exchange over the years. In brief the idea was the creation of a 'Sinking Fund' (an unhappy title), which was first propounded by Paterson of Bank of England fame and Darien notoriety. The intention was for the Commissioners for the Reduction of the National Debt to invest a sum of capital in government stock and each year thereafter the accrued interest would be reinvested until by virtue of 'interest upon interest' the entire capital debt would be discharged. The sum proposed was £250,000. A stockbroker, one Benjamin Cole, was nominated to operate the scheme with the brief not to invest more than £5000 at any one time and to buy 'at best'. Mr Cole had to reconcile this conservative philosophy with the requirement to meet the overall commitment of £250,000 invested each year. This cannot have been an easy equation to resolve and there must have been times when the market 'saw him coming'. In the event and not altogether surprisingly the scheme made very small inroads into the total burden of the National Debt. What is worth recording is that Cole became the first recognised Government Broker and that his firm, Mullens & Company, still holds the office.

But the brokers and jobbers were still looked on slightly askance. In 1733, for example, an Act was passed which had as one of its declared objects 'to prevent the infamous practice of stock-jobbing'. The Act set out pretty stringent provisions for regulating rather than actually pro-scribing the jobbers' activities, and laid down what must have been heavy penalties by way of fines for knowingly indulging in some of the less desirable practices which had undoubtedly been going on. It is possible that this most recent manifestation of a lingering disapproval in the minds of many did provide a spur for the brokers and jobbers to band more closely together, and to give their budding profession a more formal establishment.

With just such an object in mind a nucleus of brokers took the decision to establish themselves as an entity with, if not a strictly formal constitution, at least a selective membership. In this they were some years ahead of the commodity market associations. Of these founder members as they might justly if loosely be called, there were but 150, each paying a sub-scription of £8 per annum. Jonathan's was their headquarters, and thus

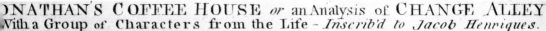

JNATHAN'S COFFEE HOUSE *or* an Analysis of CHANGE ALLEY
With a Group of Characters from the Life - *Inscrib'd to Jacob Henriques.*

Jonathan's coffee house: an engraving by H. O. Neal

things remained for a few years.

What the founders had not taken into account though was that entry into Jonathan's or indeed any coffee house was a matter of habit, and that *habitués* from worlds other than stockbroking were equally welcomed by the proprietor. It was not long therefore before the members of what at the time was little more than a club decided that Jonathan's as it stood was not for them. Without further ado they set out to find new, or at least reasonably exclusive, premises, and so was born the 'New Jonathan's' also in Threadneedle Street, to which an admission charge of sixpence daily

107

was made. At last the brokers had their own roof over their heads. With a singularly happy choice of nomenclature, it was decided in 1773 to change its name from 'New Jonathan's' to the 'Stock Exchange'. From such strokes of somebody's imagination are institutions identified for the rest of time. For a while the proprietors of the coffee house – for such it still remained – kept a position of influence along with, and on occasion in dispute with, a separate committee of the members. Not perfect, but it was a beginning.

This informal arrangement, the effect of which at the time was only to restrict membership, lasted without any significant modification until the beginning of the nineteenth century. On 7 January 1801 a resolution was passed converting the Stock Exchange into a Subscription Room. This marked the first step towards a more formal constitution. A single committee was formed out of the amalgamation of the previously existing Proprietors' and General Purposes Committees, to be known as the United Committee. This was an arrangement different from that of Lloyd's and certain of the commodity markets, which retained the distinction between management of the market and control of the logistical side. The United Committee's first chairman was Mr John Barnes. Rules were drawn up, including provision for the election of members by ballot, and the subscription was fixed at ten guineas. Thus was the Stock Exchange formally closed and the Stock Subscription Room brought into being.

One of the declared objects of this more closely regulated body was the improvement of the image of stockbroking as a profession. To this end, a measure of selectivity was necessary, though it proved unpopular with some of the rowdier members who found themselves excluded from membership of the Subscription Room. A system of fines for 'disorderly conduct' was also instituted – the proceeds, we are told, going to charity.

The offence does not appear to have been adequately defined, however, and in a short time there was serious discord on the new committee. This led to the resignation of the chairman, John Battye, and several others who supported him over a case of alleged disorderly conduct. No doubt there was more behind the lack of agreement than this particular pretext; it may well have been a matter of the 'old guard' resenting the reforming zeal of those whom they looked on as inexperienced in matters pertaining to the management of the exchange. In the event, the split was serious enough to bring about the break-up of the United Committee. After a period of some confusion which was fortunately of short duration, the new management held its first meeting (without Battye and his supporters) in March 1801 in the Antwerp tavern. This time, William Hammond took the chair, and Barnes was amongst those present.

The meeting was told that premises in Capel Court (off Bartholomew Lane) had been secured as more suitable for their needs. The building was to cost £15,000 including costs of conversion to its new use, and this was to be raised by the issue of 300 shares of £50 each. The Proprietors' Committee was advised that its members were to become owners of 100 of the shares. This gesture to the old guard was not well received, however, and the old Proprietors brusquely refused the offer.

As in present times, so in 1801. The estimated cost of buying and re-furbishing the Capel Court building rose in a very short time from £15,000 to £20,000. It was also found that more land was needed, and so the gym-nasium of the bare-fist boxer Mendoza had to go and the neighbouring Hercules tavern found itself adapted to serve the dual purpose of second entrance and members' bar. This second doorway gave access from Throg-morton Street via Hercules Court. The new building followed classic bourse practice with a large and lofty trading room where specialists in the various markets were soon to establish their own 'pitch', which included one for the National Debt – forerunner of the gilt-edged market.

The foundation stone – of copper – was laid on 15 May 1801. It was uncovered almost accidentally in 1883 during excavation work for the construction of new vaults and found to have the interesting inscription that '. . . being the first year of the union between Great Britain and Ireland the Public Funded Debt had accumulated in five successive years to £582,730,924.' The message made reference to the Constitution and ended with the words 'May the blessings of that Constitution be transmitted to the latest Posterity'. Along with Peacock, the architect, the names of the founders were also inscribed on the copper.

At this time a list of the stocks dealt in included only the 'English Funds' (what today would be called government stocks) and occasional supporting lotteries. There appears not to have been a market there in shares in joint-stock companies as such, whilst foreign funds were still traded in the Royal Exchange.

We should recall here that the reorganisation and the opening of the new rooms took place against the background of the war with France. The City was nervous: rumours abounded concerning the progress of the war and these inevitably had their effect on the prices of quoted funds. It was a situation not dissimilar to that which briefly obtained in 1745 when Prince Charles Edward Stuart and his Highlanders had marched as far south as Derby at the peak of the 'Forty-five' uprising – a relatively recent event. There had already been a considerable outburst of panic selling in

The New Stock Exchange: aquatint by Pugin and Rowlandson

1797 due to a rumour that the French had landed – this time in Wales. Such rumours were not unusual and were taken far more seriously than their content would seem to warrant, but we have to bear in mind that communications were slow and news lent itself to exaggeration by repetition in the relaying of messages. In 1797 selling resulting from the invasion rumour was enough to depress 3 per cent Consols from $97\frac{1}{4}$ to $47\frac{3}{8}$. In 1803 an optimistic report (subsequently found to have been a fabrication) anticipating the signing of the Treaty of Amiens pushed the funds from $63\frac{3}{4}$ to $71\frac{1}{4}$. This time, the Committee closed the Exchange pending confirmation of the report. On its exposure as a forgery they declared all bargains void, and offered a reward for the apprehension of its author.

In 1814 the victory of the Battle of Waterloo was anticipated by the spreading of a rumour that Napoleon had been killed and Paris sacked. This was the work of a singularly enterprising coterie, one of whose members actually staged a dramatic arrival at Dover and dash to London with the news – which he was careful to retail to any listener *en route*. In the event there was a public enquiry into the affair, which was held on the insistence of the Committee of the Stock Exchange. Admiral Cochrane was accused of involvement in the plot and was disgraced, though his guilt is rather hard to credit in view of his record, and the relative smallness of any financial gain he may have made on the upsurge of prices which took place. The other legend, that of the Rothschild coup with carrier pigeons after Waterloo had indeed been fought in 1815, is almost certainly apocryphal.

As to the management of the young Stock Exchange and how the rules governing membership and conduct emerged, we go back a little in time – noting *inter alia* that membership was originally limited to 500 rather than taking the risk of affording 'new facilities to the criminal designs of notorious and unprincipled gamblers'. The first codification of what were to become the Rules of the Stock Exchange was the outcome of the discovery that the secretary in these formative years had been less than efficient in keeping records of meetings and decisions taken at them. A subcommittee was set up, with as its brief a complete review of all the Committee records and their editing into something less diffuse than the mass of papers through which they had to sift. They were successful, and in February 1812 the General Purposes Committee approved their synopsis and adopted it as what was to be the foundation of today's Rules of the Stock Exchange.

We have already noted that business in foreign loans was conducted in the Royal Exchange, but this situation was soon to be altered. During the years of war preceding Waterloo, many quite sizeable loans had been raised by the London merchant banks, notable amongst them in this context being Barings and Rothschilds. A British house, Boyd, Benfield & Company, had also been active in the business but met with misfortune when a loan to the Austrian government proved an expensive failure. In 1822 six Stock Exchange members were moved to write to the Committee requesting that a market in foreign securities be instituted, which they felt would afford 'great convenience and profit to the House at large'. The six attracted much support amongst their fellow members. Their efforts were rewarded in October of that year by a favourable decision of the Committee. There were problems still to be solved though, in connection with the Rules and their interpretation, for it was not until 1823 that the Foreign Stock Market Committee was set up and membership of this market within a market regularised. With the end of the boom in foreign issues the Foreign Stock Exchange ceased to occupy its own room and the separation of the two markets was discontinued.

The railway boom came and went, dominated by the enigmatic figure of George Hudson. Spurred on by a sense of urgency occasioned by the rush of new flotations, the government grappled with the problems of regulating company matters. One outcome of its efforts was that the Companies Act 1844 laid down that all new joint-stock companies be registered and finally in 1862 the principle of the limited liability company was once and for all established. However, this provision did not at the time apply to the joint-stock banks. We have read in Chapter 3 of the collapse in 1878 of the City of Glasgow Bank, which came as the culmination of a series of smaller bank failures over the preceding quarter-century. This disastrous failure was to prove the end of the era of unlimited liability amongst the banks and the Companies Act 1879 converted the whole of the banking sector to the comparatively new limited liability concept.

As to the Stock Exchange itself, by 1850 it was becoming uncomfortably crowded in the 1802 building. The decision was taken to double the extent of available accommodation, and William Cubitt, of Belgravia renown, was commissioned to build it to the design of Thomas Allason. During the building operations the members moved into temporary quarters in the Hall of Commerce in Threadneedle Street, but their stay there was a remarkably short one, the new Exchange being actually ready for occupation in early 1854. Within twenty years this building, too, was severely overcrowded, notwithstanding the conversion in 1872 of its basement restaurant – Mabey's – into the settling-room. Membership now totalled 2000, and something had to be done. Therefore in 1884 the New House was opened and occupied. It covered an area next to the Old House, as the earlier building had come to be known. The New House was soon dubbed Gorgonzola Hall, in reference to the veined marble with which it was copiously decorated. It was in these ornate surroundings that the Stock Exchange continued to broaden its scope. The 'Kaffir Circus', as the market in gold-mining and finance house shares was disrespectfully nicknamed, arrived with the exploitation of the deposits buried deep under the Rand. Two world wars and the intervening world boom and slump brought their share of 'triumph and disaster' – happily with the emphasis on the former.

And so to the present day and the twenty-six storey tower which now houses the Exchange as well as providing house-room for a number of other institutions. The demolition of Gorgonzola Hall and the erection of the new building, of which the foundation stone was laid by Her Majesty

The American market at the Stock Exchange, drawn by Lockhart Bogle

the Queen Mother in 1967, were so phased as to permit trading to continue uninterrupted. The new tower was formally opened by Her Majesty the Queen on 8 November 1972.

In the concluding chapter we shall consider some of the more important recent events and trends which have, or are likely to have, a major influence on the Stock Exchange and possibly even on the whole rationale of public investment. Meanwhile, the essential adaptability of this particular 'city within the City' serves as a continuing reassurance to the very many who are in one way or another involved – whether as investors in their own right or vicariously as participants in a pension fund or as policyholders in an insurance company.

CHAPTER NINE

Looking Towards Tomorrow

One of the most difficult tasks facing anybody bold or foolish enough to attempt to set down a history of a living and contemporary thing such as the City, is where to make the cut-off point?, where to close the book and say with justification 'that's it, as far as it goes'?

We have seen examples in earlier chapters of trends beginning to develop, which are continuing and which have a profound influence on the direction in which the story will proceed; upon what will be history this time to-morrow. In our story there is really no cut-off point. So, in these final pages let us take up the threads of some of these developments, especially those where the different sectors are showing more signs of direct influence upon each other. The chief areas where this is happening are in banking and investment, with the latter in turn affected by growth in the insurance sector.

We have already paid some attention to what we have described as 'wholesale banking' (see Chapter 4), and to the reconstitution of the British overseas banks with such business in view. Now we should see just how the whole notion of lending on such a scale has crystallised and how it has brought into being a quite new market, one which in particular has had a profound effect upon the operation – and the numbers – of the foreign banks established in the City. The coming of the foreign banks was an inflow different both in nature and cause from the earlier arrivals here of European nationals who set themselves up in London. These were, almost without exception, people who wished, for various and often personal reasons, to establish domicile here. Over the years they have become an important part of the City and today they are no more 'foreign' than any of the native-born institutions. More English than the English, perhaps.

The more recently arrived foreign banks retain both their identities and their nationalities. Though generally apt, the word 'recent' in this context should be qualified in some instances; for example the Moscow Narodny Bank has been in the City since 18 October 1919. However, the majority are new arrivals and their combined influence – and competition – is a relatively new phenomenon. It is certainly one which has given a fresh stimulus to the banking side of the City and which has probably been the biggest single justification for its claim still to be the foremost banking and financial centre in the world. It is said, and with some justification, that over one half of the City's invisible earnings are attributable to the activities of the foreign banks.

There are two main reasons for the currently strong position of these friendly invaders, amongst whom numerically the Americans are in the majority, though now in company with a strong Japanese contingent. The first reason, and that which goes most of the way towards accounting for the high proportion of American banks among the City's newer residents, is simply that these institutions found it worth their while opening offices here in order to service the needs of their own compatriots. The end of the Second World War left many American organisations with at least one military, or quasi-military foot in Europe – so why not place the other, commercial, foot there too? As a natural consequence American banks began to set themselves up in London, as Europe's financial centre, with the main aim of servicing the requirements of the subsidiaries or sister-companies of US corporations.

The second reason is to be found in our own British banking regulations which were in force in the earlier post-war years. At the time, these regulations prevented the clearing banks from participating in wholesale, or money-market banking, involving large sums out on short- to medium-term loan. In order, therefore, to gain entry into what they saw to be a most attractive market it was necessary for the clearers to set up specialist subsidiaries. This was costly, and it took quite a measure of innovatory nerve to make such a major break from traditional methods. In consequence, the arrival on the scene of the British clearing banks in this particular guise happened only after many foreign banks were already well-established there.

As to the more specialised London banks, typically the merchant banks, who were not bound by any such restrictions, there were individual problems such as commitments in other fields and, in the final count, lack of sheer size to deal from their own unaided resources in the sort of sums by that time involved.

The restrictions on wholesale lending by the clearing banks were eventually lifted in 1971, when a whole new set of controls was introduced and it now remains to be seen to what extent the giant clearers, many with their

The Moscow Narodny Bank in King William Street

own newly established merchant banking subsidiaries, are taking advantage of the opportunities thus offered. We shall also see how their competition (which surely must grow inexorably) will affect the position of the foreign banks who did have a lead in the field. On the other side of the ledger, as it were, there are increasing signs of the American banks in particular making inroads into retail, or over-the-counter banking in Britain. This two-way competition may well be beneficial to customers of the banks, but confronts them all – both British and foreign – with its own problems of economy and overhead costs.

The consortium bank and the syndicated loan were two new concepts brought into being in order to deal with the problem of scale which was now becoming a pressing one. As to the former, it was generally with one of the American banks that others would collaborate so as to achieve a capital base broad enough to cope with the sort of figures which were becoming the rule rather than the exception. (Though a bank's deposits are its main source of funds available for lending, it has to be borne in mind that sufficient deposits would be unlikely to be attracted were the financial foundations of the bank not seen to be adequate in size and strength.) An example of a consortium bank is Orion, which comprises the National Westminster Bank, the Chase Manhattan, the West Deutscher Landesbank, the Royal Bank of Canada, Mitsubishi Bank and Credito Italiano.

Up to a point therefore such very large consortia are well able to lend many millions from their combined resources. It may yet be necessary, though, to provide even greater sums and with the complications attendant upon more than one loan of such magnitude being sought at the same time. The syndicated loan is another way of attempting to deal with this problem. Here the practice generally is for the 'lead bank' to maintain contact with the borrower, discussing the proposition with other banks (in a way not dissimilar from the operation of the Lloyd's broker) and, when amount and terms are agreed, the lead bank returns to the borrower with the offer.

Why should it be that scope for transactions on such a scale has arisen at all? The cause lies largely in the emergence of a quite new 'eurocurrency' business in which the sums involved may be truly vast, even after making allowance for the general devaluation of most currencies in real terms. With the spread of nationalisation has arrived the large public utility corporation – the electricity generating board and the state-owned railways board are examples – which along with other giants in the multinational sector are increasingly seeking medium-term funds in this area.

The origins of the eurocurrency market can be traced back to 1958, when convertibility of sterling was reinstituted after the Second World War. At about this time large quantities of US dollars had found their way into Europe in the course of ordinary commercial activity, and there was a serious disincentive to their repatriation. This was due to the then current American regulations restricting interest rates in the USA. Consequently, banks in Europe and especially in the City of London were in a position to attract these 'exiled' US funds by offering rates of interest on them which appeared generous in comparison with those which the New York and other American domestic banks were able to provide. London had a peculiar relevance in this situation because pressure on sterling had resulted in the imposition of restrictions on the financing of third-country trade in pounds. Thus, the surplus dollars were seized on as a most opportune alternative. Additionally, foreign borrowers, including for this purpose such expatriates as overseas subsidiaries of US companies, turned to the European market for the satisfaction of their ordinary borrowing needs; being deterred, indeed virtually barred, from using New York by the restrictive effect of American government controls such as an Interest Equalisation Tax then in force.

So, a combination of financial restrictions in New York and pressure on sterling in Britain was taken as the opportunity for an exercise in ingenuity which has resulted in the establishment of this new, though by now quite accepted, market in medium-term lending.

The US dollar remains the most-used currency in the eurocurrency market, but it is by no means the only one. Any denomination can be brought into the net as a 'euro' currency when it is owned by a non-resident of its country of issue – hence one of the attractions to the American banks in establishing European offshoots. Being, in this context, of European domicile such subsidiaries may deal in the eurodollar market and, should occasion demand, make eurodollar loans to their own parents. Hence too the American invasion of London and of Moorgate in particular – to the extent that it is sometimes jocularly referred to as the 'Avenue of the Americas'.

Stemming from the success of eurodollar business (and sharing the same original *raison d'être*) other new markets are in course of evolution. Of these the eurobond method of raising longer-term finance by the issue of bonds underwritten by a consortium of banks is by now fairly well established, though London has not as yet achieved a really major share of this market. This is chiefly because domestic UK exchange control regulations inhibit British investors from subscribing to bond issues in eurocurrencies. It is an apt comment on the continuing war between the regulation makers and the financial and commercial 'free marketeers' that out of a set of no doubt well-intentioned and (at the time) necessary restrictions a whole new financial concept has been born. This is a field in which we shall undoubtedly see many further developments.

If the eurodollar market and the consortium bank are having their influence on the structure of the banking section of the City, other forces are at work which are bringing about a sort of sea-change in the area of investment. Chief among these is the emergence of the institutional investor to the point where he is – in the opinion of some – coming to have perhaps too strong an influence over the stock market. Life assurance companies, pension funds and unit trusts have each in their various ways caused investment decisions to be taken by fewer people and at the same time placed very much larger funds in relatively fewer hands. This is all a part of the same process that we have noted in the context of banking and the development of the very large unit in that sphere.

We have already seen how the spread of the notion of life assurance has built a considerable financial structure upon the foundation of the original mutual and other societies. In like manner, the pension fund for the employees of a company or group of companies has developed into a very large corporate investor indeed. (Pension funds have actually been looking at other outlets for their funds of late, making investment purchases of property and even of works of art.) Along with these two growing corporate investors and in some instances sharing similar special tax arrangements – which affects the choice of investment – the unit trusts have proliferated.

The first records of a unit trust in England date from 1868, and *The Times* of the day summarised its objects neatly: 'for enabling the public to make investments in foreign and colonial securities without encountering the risks incidental to any individual purchase'. In theory this was fair comment. In practice it has been found necessary to regulate the activities of unit trust promoters and to separate the 'authorised' trusts which may advertise for subscriptions from others where general advertisement is not permitted. The basis of such distinction lies in the facility or otherwise for a regular valuation of the underlying assets of the trust – stock exchange quoted securities for example are readily and regularly valued whereas property and other such assets present problems in this context. The movement towards these 'open-ended' funds developed first in the USA and the first major operation along these lines in this country was Municipal and General Securities ('M & G'), which has since been joined by a whole bevy of trusts. Essentially, by buying units in a fund of which buyers' and sellers' prices are regularly quoted, the investor can put his money into a basket of securities giving a useful spread of risk, or giving the *entrée* into one or more specialised areas suited to his tax situation or other particular need.

All of these comparatively recently arrived corporate investors have jointly had a considerable influence on the securities market, to the extent that there are now voices bemoaning the demise of the proverbial 'widows and orphans'. In fact, both are still with us – personal taxation permitting – but many are now aggregated into the body of holders of units in a trust or are vicarious investors as payers of insurance premiums or beneficiaries under a pension fund.

Ever larger, more international and numerically fewer, these more recent creations deal habitually in far greater sums than did the whole of the nineteenth century City's body of lenders, borrowers and investors. With the exception of Lloyd's, and in particular the commodity markets whose membership remains almost anachronistically fragmented, the present and foreseeable development of the City is towards bigger units, each becoming more closely linked to complementary bodies in other hitherto specialised fields of operation.

In the course of this process, the older traditional boundaries between one specialisation and another are becoming blurred. True, there remain some areas which appear to be inviolate – the discount houses for example, though reduced in numbers, pursue their calling, and maintain their relationship with the Bank of England in their own very special way. The multifarious brokerage houses are still for the most part independent, and tend to concentrate their activities in one or a few fields. But these are, one might say, the exceptions which prove the rule. The very nature of their business is such that amalgamation, save with others in the same line of business, is fraught with difficulty. Where such obstacles are not present the tendency towards groupings of complementary activities – without going so far as the not very happy 'conglomerates' containing disparate activities within one group – becomes ever more apparent.

It appears – and this is a fortunate thing – that this development is taking place without undue depersonalisation of the various institutions. So much of the City's comparative success has rested, as we have seen in earlier chapters, on the role of the individual who has authority to enter into commitments without the need for excessively bureaucratic procedures. Where committees do operate, they are small. If the computer has assumed much of the statistician's and the clerk's functions, it has so far been confined to these tasks (and it still has to be programmed by skilful human beings) and is not so revered as to be attributed with powers it does not possess. Training, and the 'nose' for a sound deal remain paramount.

It is more from other directions than the tendency to coalesce that any serious threat to the traditional and proven *modus operandi* may yet come. Both national and, to an increasing degree, supra-national bureaucracy, in the form especially of the EEC directorate, do on occasion pose problems for those whose whole ethic is to keep formality and protocol within the strictest of limits. In this context the Bank of England plays its own very vital part as a link between Westminster and the City. Though the Bank's actual status was altered by the 1946 Act which virtually nationalised it, successive governments have nevertheless accepted it for what it always was. This has without doubt smoothed the path of any dialogue between the two areas of political and financial activity. With the increasingly international emphasis on the work of the City's institutions the continuance of such a dialogue can only assume ever greater importance. Flexibility and adaptability are the keystones of any successful financial edifice, and these are qualities not often found in over-elaborate legislation or bureaucratic procedures.

From the standpoint of those outside it, yet whose business activities (be they corporate or individually as investor or borrower) bring them into frequent contact with the City, what does this complicated and rather specialised machine actually produce by way of benefit to us, as components

The Bank of England

of the nation at large? How may the machine's output be quantified in terms of profit and loss in the country's books?

Such questions must have been asked, and much speculation indulged in as to their answers, for many years. It is a somewhat surprising thing, therefore, to find that only comparatively recently has a serious search for a definitive answer been initiated. (This is the more surprising, too, in view of the traditional interest and activity in entrepreneurial pursuits.) The instrument created for carrying out this search, or research, is the Committee on Invisible Exports. It is no reflection on this body to remark that its youth is of itself surprising – one should be the more thankful that it is now established and increasing its influence.

It could with much justification be said that invisible earnings are what the City is all about. For Britain in her heyday as a trading and manufacturing nation to have earned for herself the soubriquet 'workshop of the world', her industrialists and exporters had to be supported by all the strands in the web – shipping, finance, insurance and markets for the pricing and distribution of essential raw materials. Add to these the more recent service industries of promotion, communications and even tourism and the machinery for the expansion of trade and of foreign currency earnings is complete.

The COIE was founded in 1968, following the report of a committee which had been set up on the suggestion of the British National Export Council. This report confirmed the importance to the country's balance of payments of the so-called 'invisible exports', and it went further in recommending ways and means of actually promoting them in a practical sense. The first task of the newly established COIE was to identify all sources of invisible earnings, to obtain as precise statistics as possible, and then to spread the gospel of recognising them for what they are – significant contributions to the trading fortunes of the country. With the help of the Bank of England and the Central Statistical Office the figures were soon forthcoming and presented in a readily comprehensible form – itself no easy task in view of the very nature of invisibles.

In terms of promotion, the COIE has followed a continuing policy of encouraging, and organising, a series of two-way visits of British exporters to centres abroad and of overseas nationals to the City; conferences, seminars and informal discussions all play their part in this most important exercise.

Statistics can be liars and in any case have the unfortunate habit of becoming out of date from the very moment they are published. Just the same, there are figures which indicate in a telling way just how the City's own contribution to Britain's invisibles has grown over the years. At the inception of the COIE in 1968 the City's total was £419 millions. Just ten years later in 1977 it was £1,747 millions. Many factors have played their part in this success story; not least amongst them being the increasing recognition worldwide of London as a provider of the whole gamut of financial services from banking and insurance through commodity markets to the entrepreneurial ability of the shippers and merchants.

What more remains to be said? We have followed the progress of the City of London from its origins as a fortunately-placed centre of communications and trading to its present status as an international financial centre, which is still without rival. We have seen how native-born enterprise and ability married happily with complementary skills brought in by generations of newcomers from foreign lands and, in particular, we have seen how the gifts of ingenuity and imaginativeness have been put to good use in the evolution of new techniques and the adaptation of older ones.

As to the future, in a changing world where it becomes ever more difficult (though never impossible) to compete in the fields of production and manufacturing with both established and newly-emergent nations, one must hope that the City's own unique ability is given continued and full scope for deployment.

Index

Royal Exchange, 28, 52, 61, 65, 77, 101, 102, 109, 111
Royal Exchange Assurance Company, 80, 82
Royal Mint, 36, 37, 101
Rubber Exchange, 64, 69, 70
Rubber Growers' Association, 69
Rubber Settlement House, 70
Rubber Trade Association, 69

St Katharine's Dock, 32
St Paul's Cathedral, 14, 15
Saxons, 14, 16, 23, 34
Scottish Widows Fund, 81
'South Sea Bubble', 103, 104, 105
'South Sea Bubble Act', 80, 82, 103, 105
South Sea House, 72
Soya bean meal futures market, 68
Staple, the, 23
Steelyard, 24
Stock Exchange, 9, 49, 61, 98–114
Stock Exchange, *Official List,* 103
Sufferance wharves, 28
Sugar market, 68, 69
Sun Alliance & London Assurance Company, 79
Sun Fire Office, 79
Surrey Docks, 30
Syndicated loans, 118

Thames, river, 9, 11, 21–33
Tilbury Docks, 33
Tooley Street fire, 82

Tower Bridge, 32
Tower of London, 17, 28
Treasury, 45
Tripartite Agreement, 53

Underwriters, 74, 75, 87–97
Union Fire Insurance Office, 79
Unit trusts, 120
United Dominions Trust, 71
United States banks, 117, 118
United Terminal Sugar Market Association, 69

Vehicle and General Assurance Company, 84
Venetians, 48
Venice, 35
Victoria, Queen, 61
Virginia Coffee House, 72

Wardmoot, 16
Warehouse warrants, 61, 62
Wessex, 16
West Indies, 30, 31, 68
West Saxons, 15
Westminster Abbey, 17, 35
Westminster Bridge, 11
Westminster Fire Office, 79
William I, King, 15, 17, 34
William III, King, 37
Wood Street, 13, 19
Wool market, 71
Workmen's Compensation Act, 82, 84